Copyright © 2020 by
Unique Designs Print

All rights reserved. No part of this publication may be reproduced, distributed, or transmitted in any form or by any means, without the permission of the publisher.

This book belongs to:

_____
_____
_____

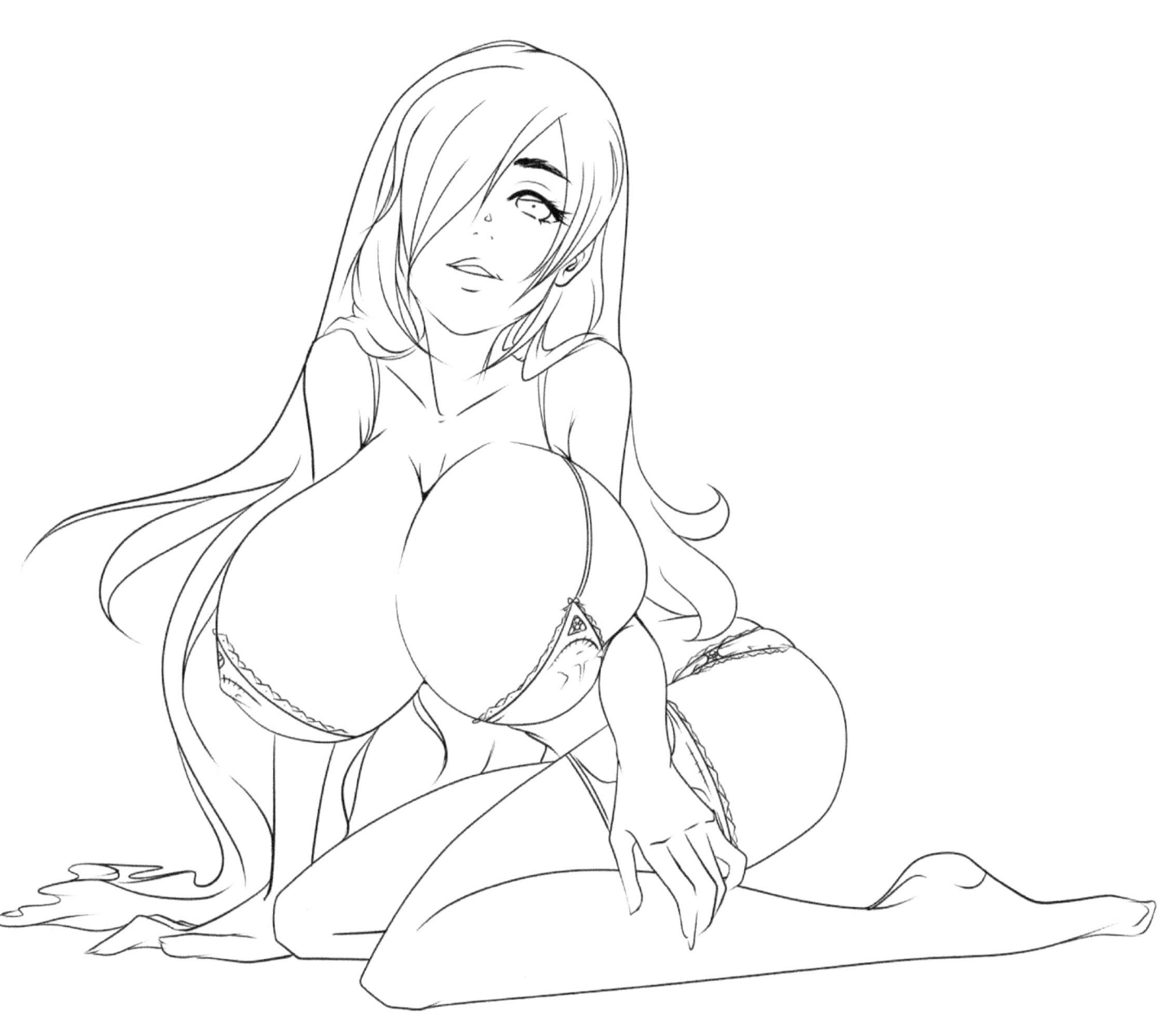

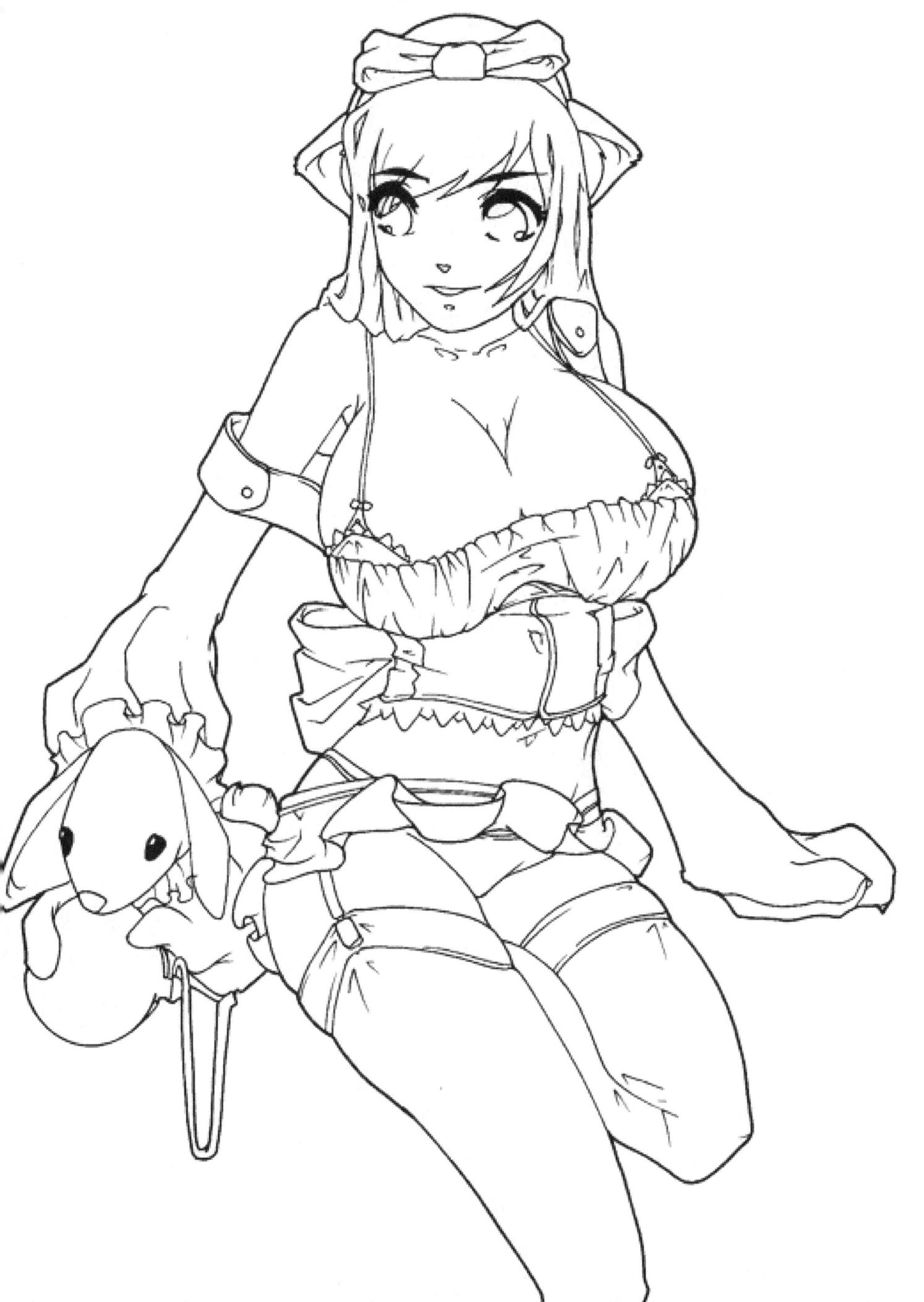

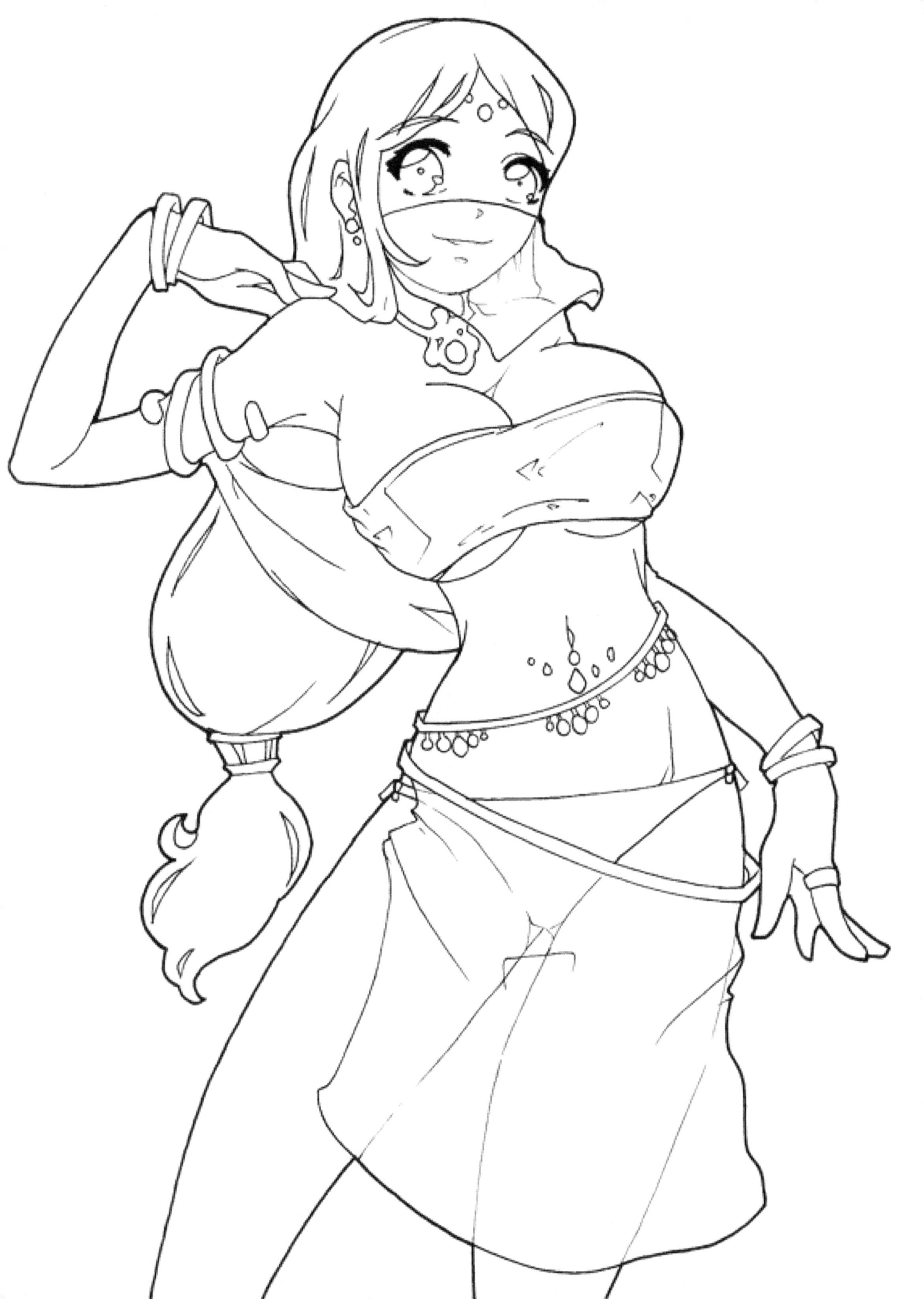

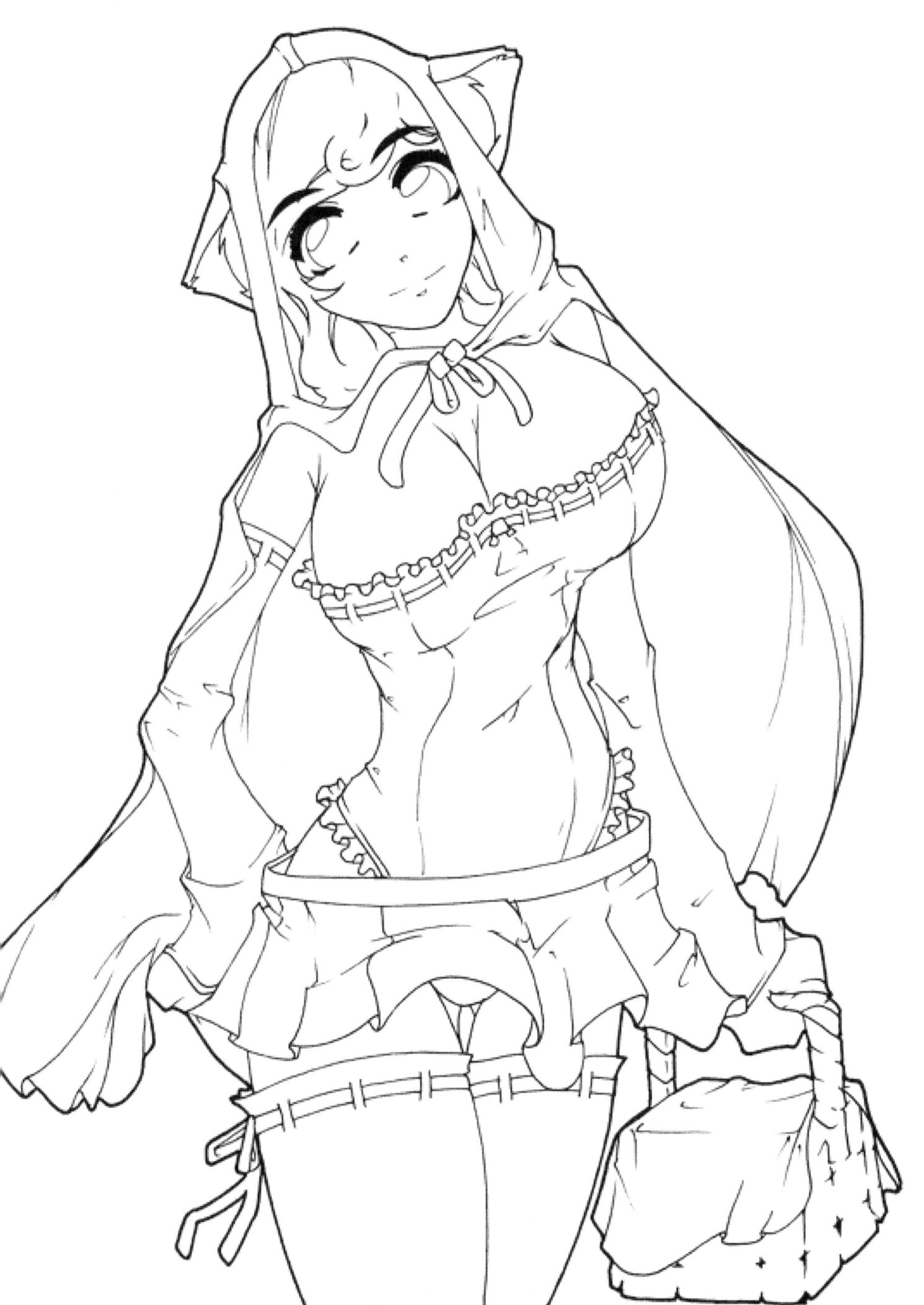

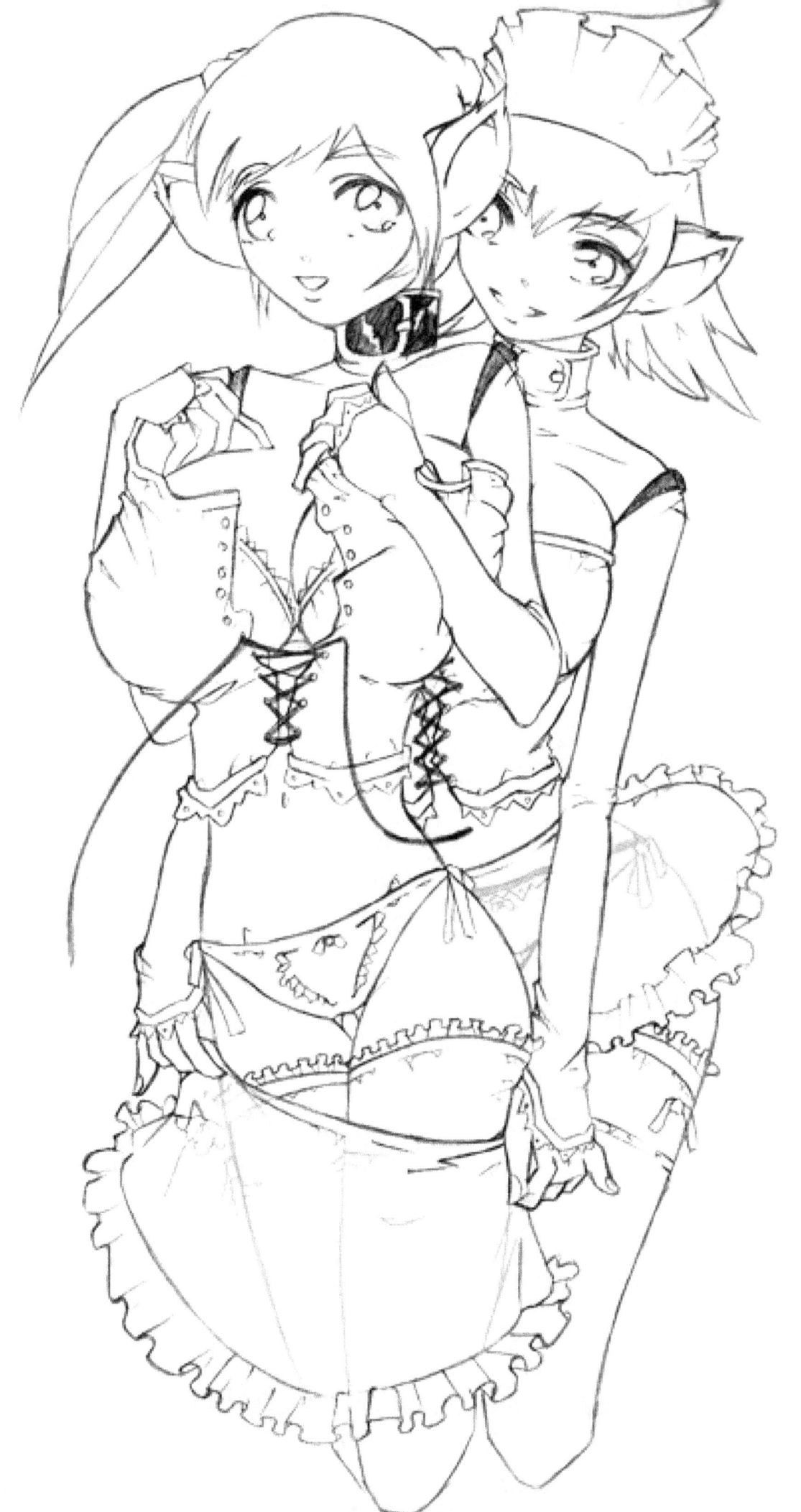

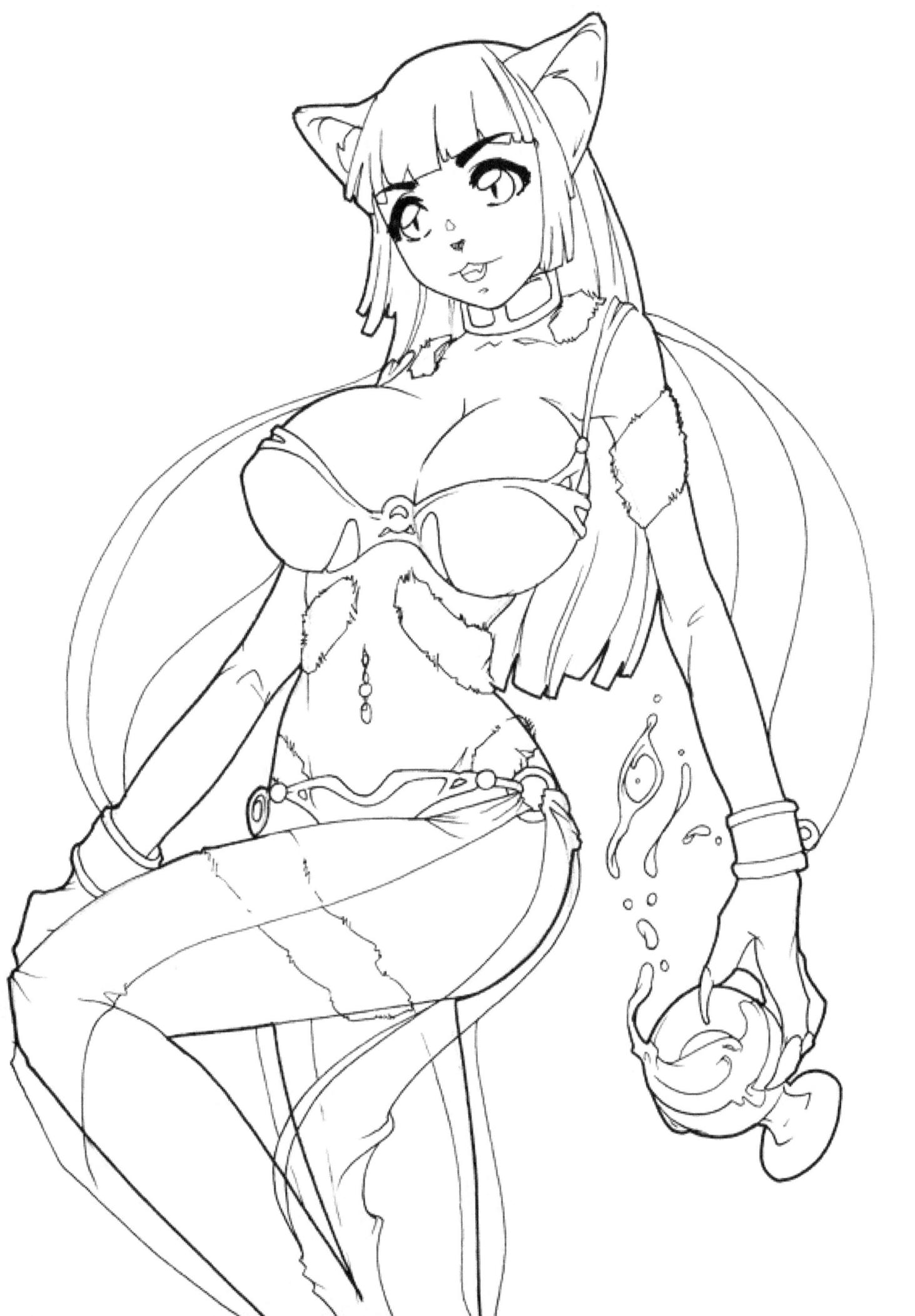

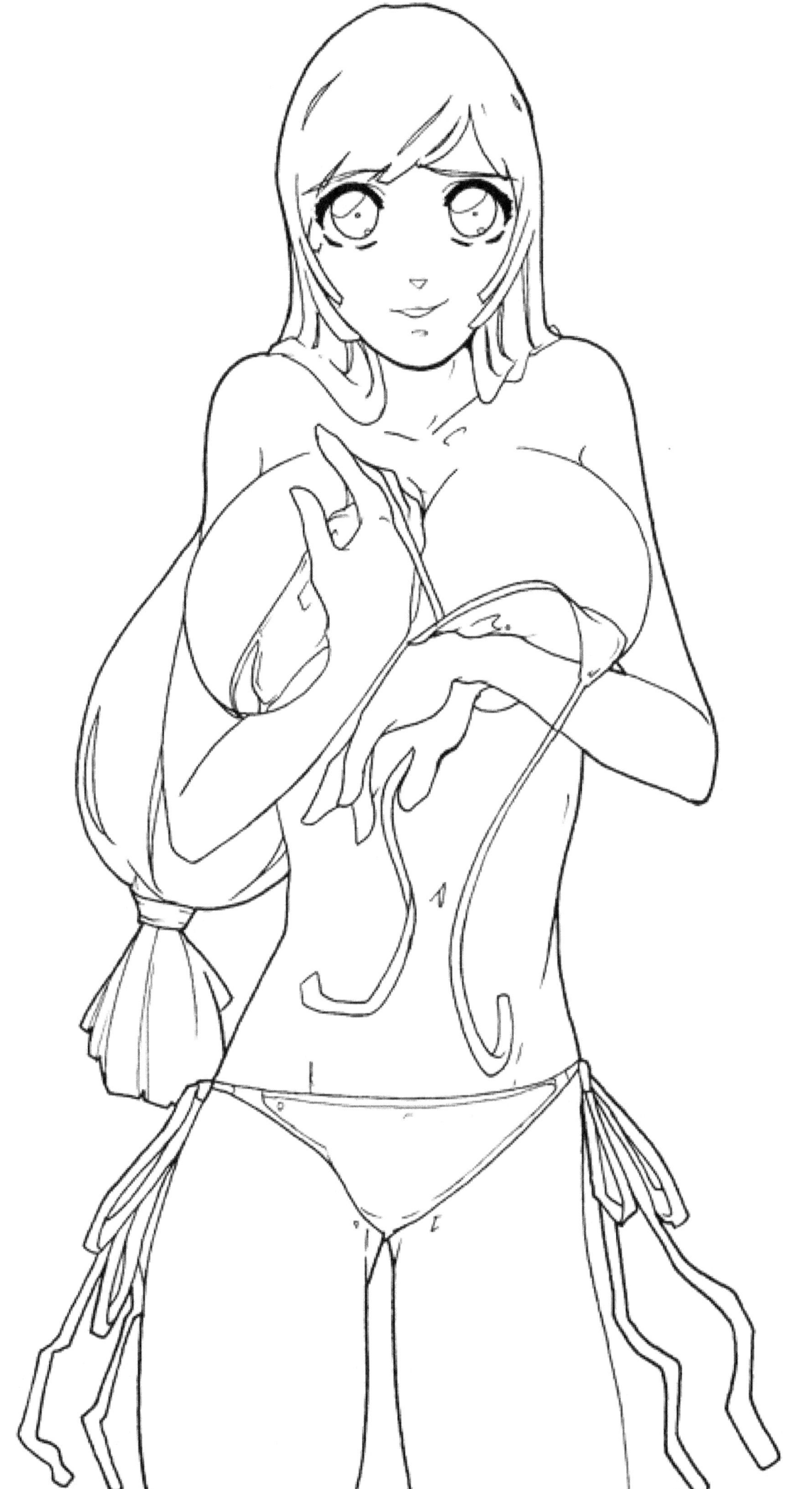

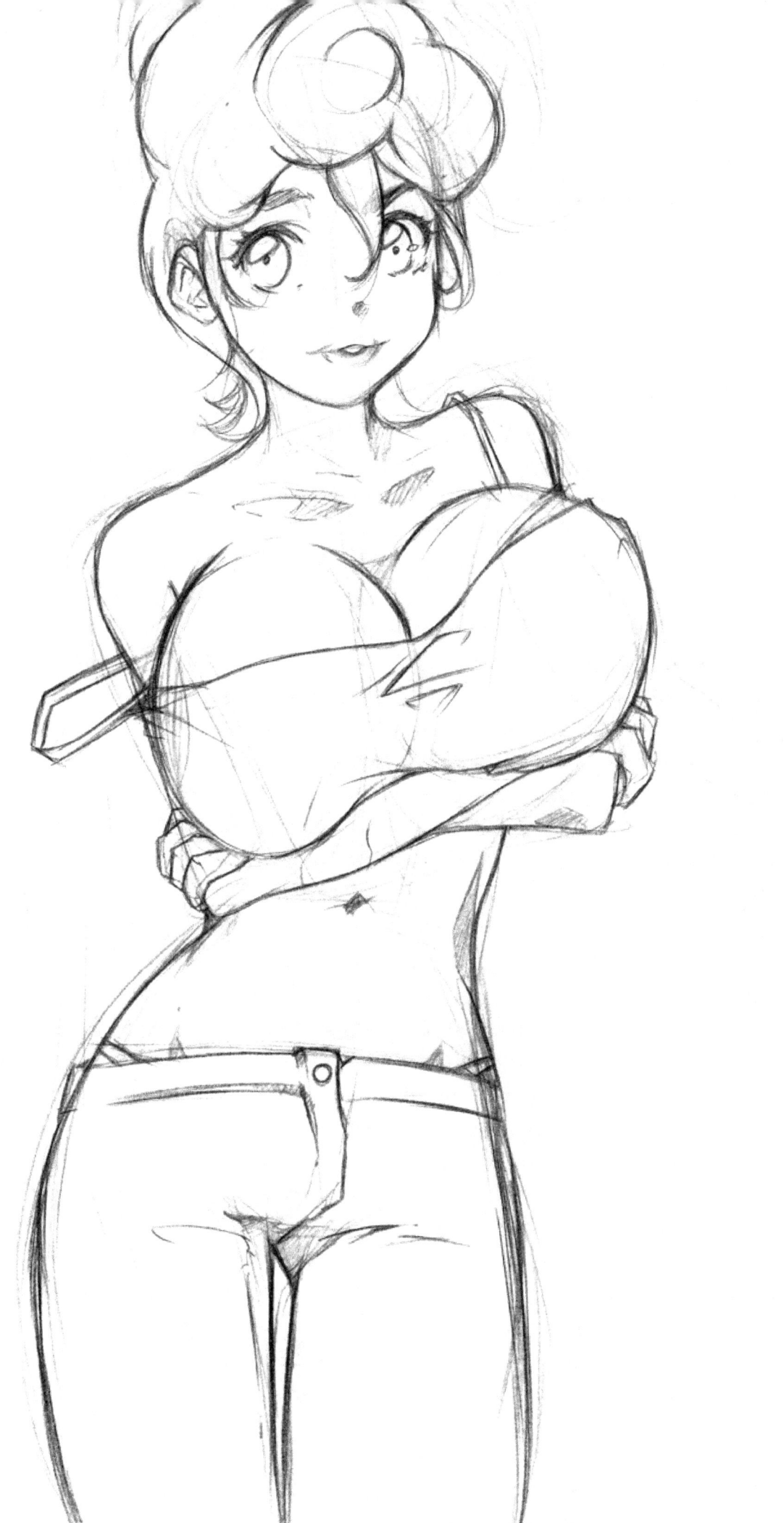

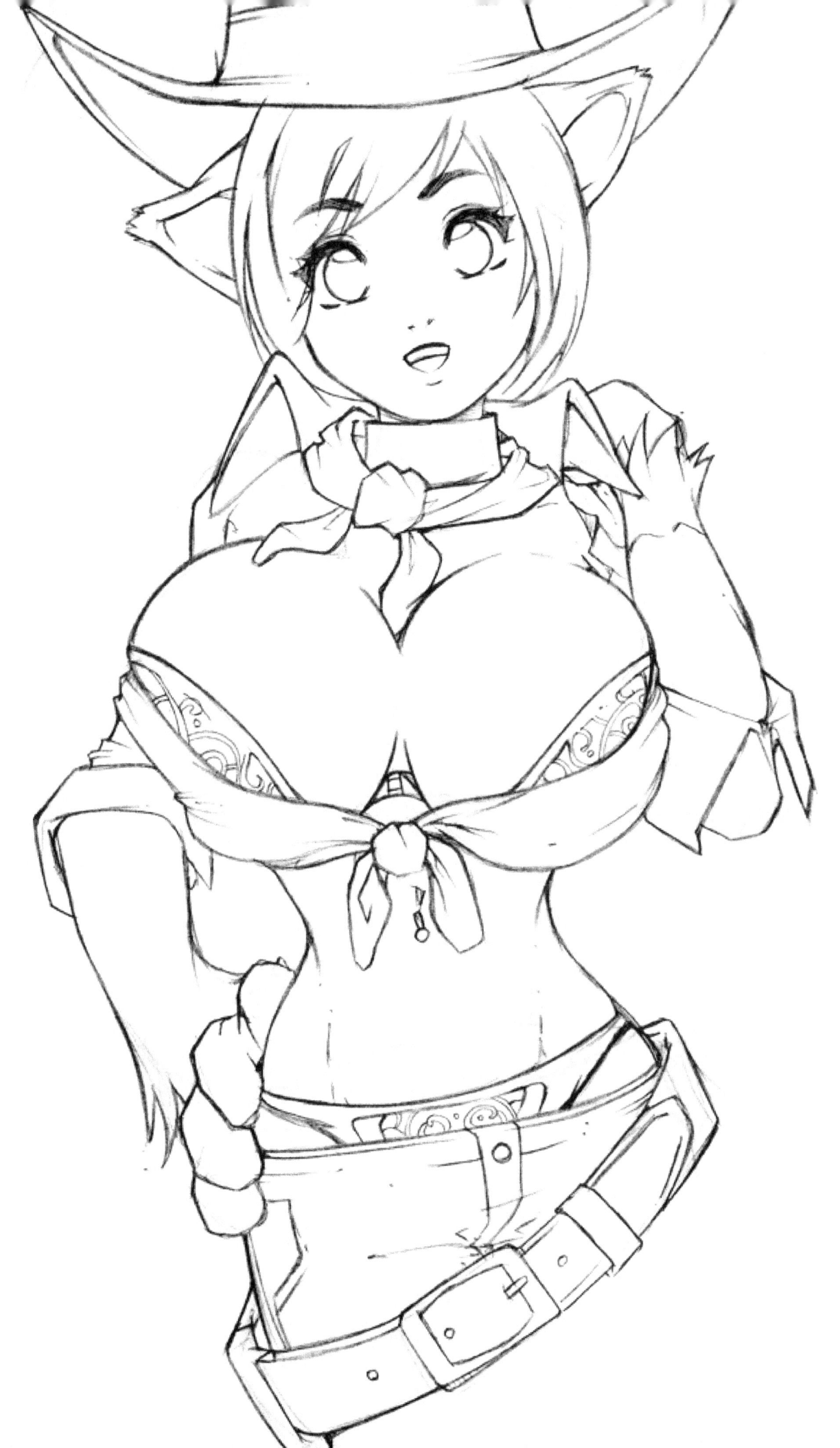

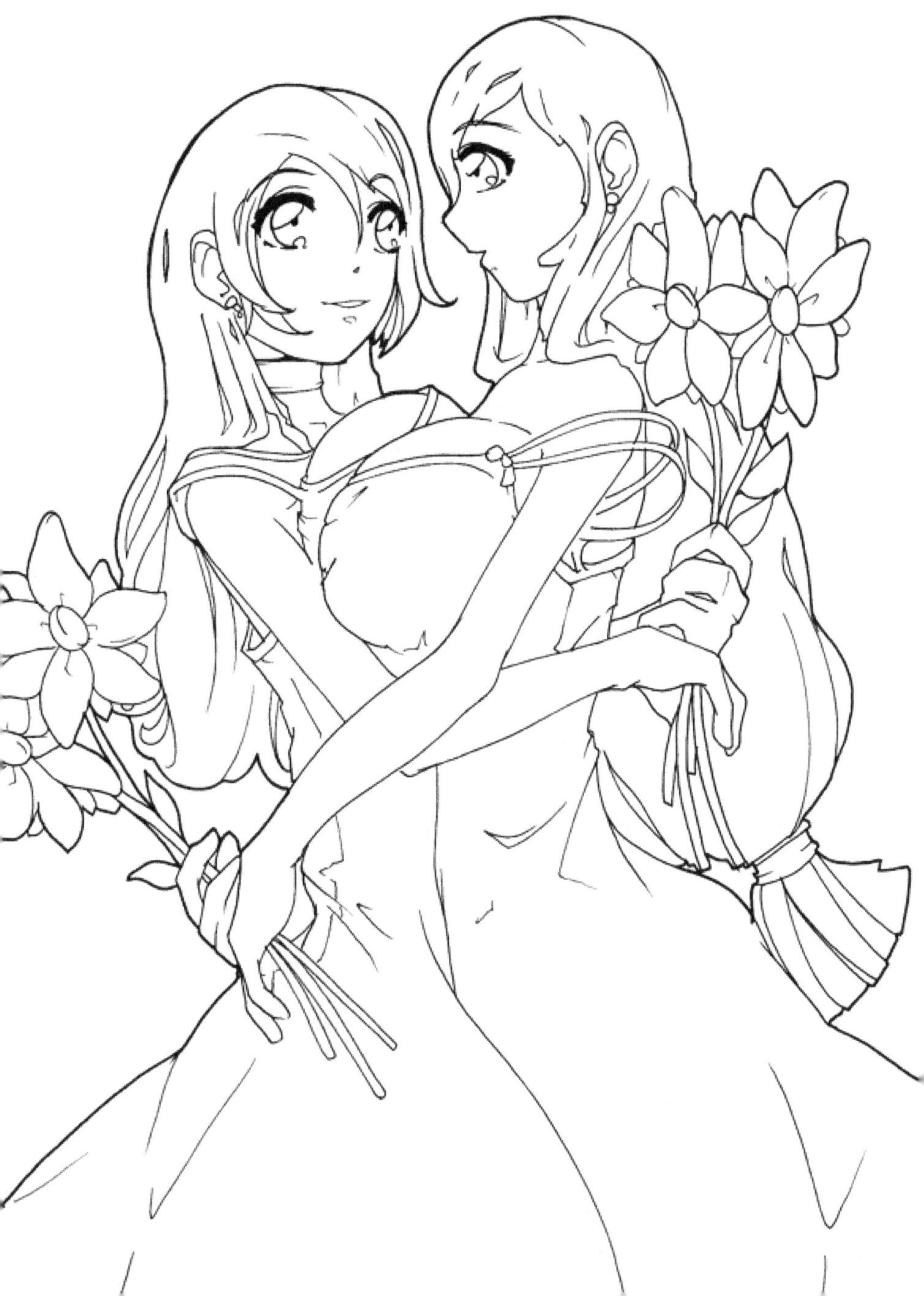

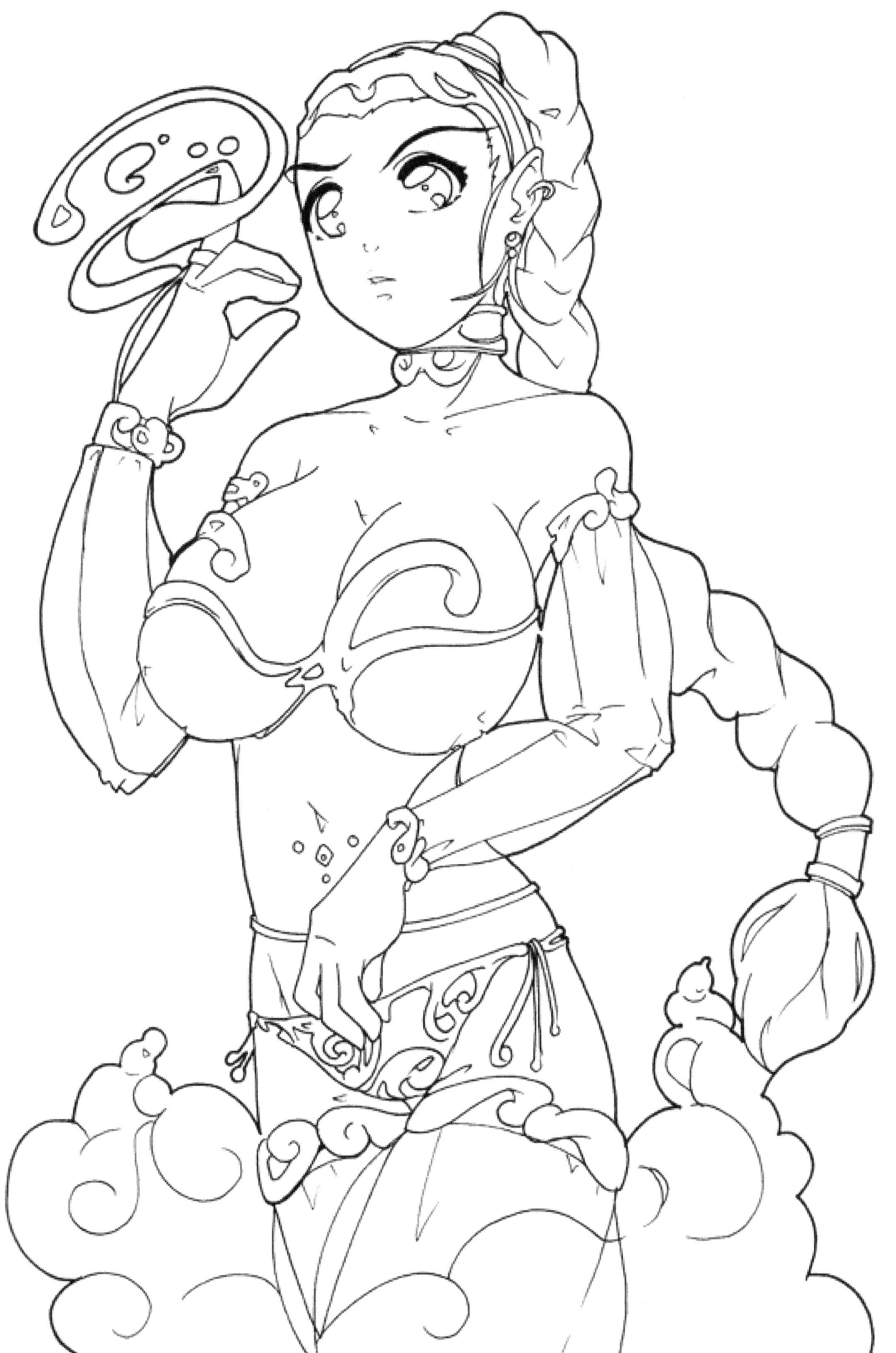

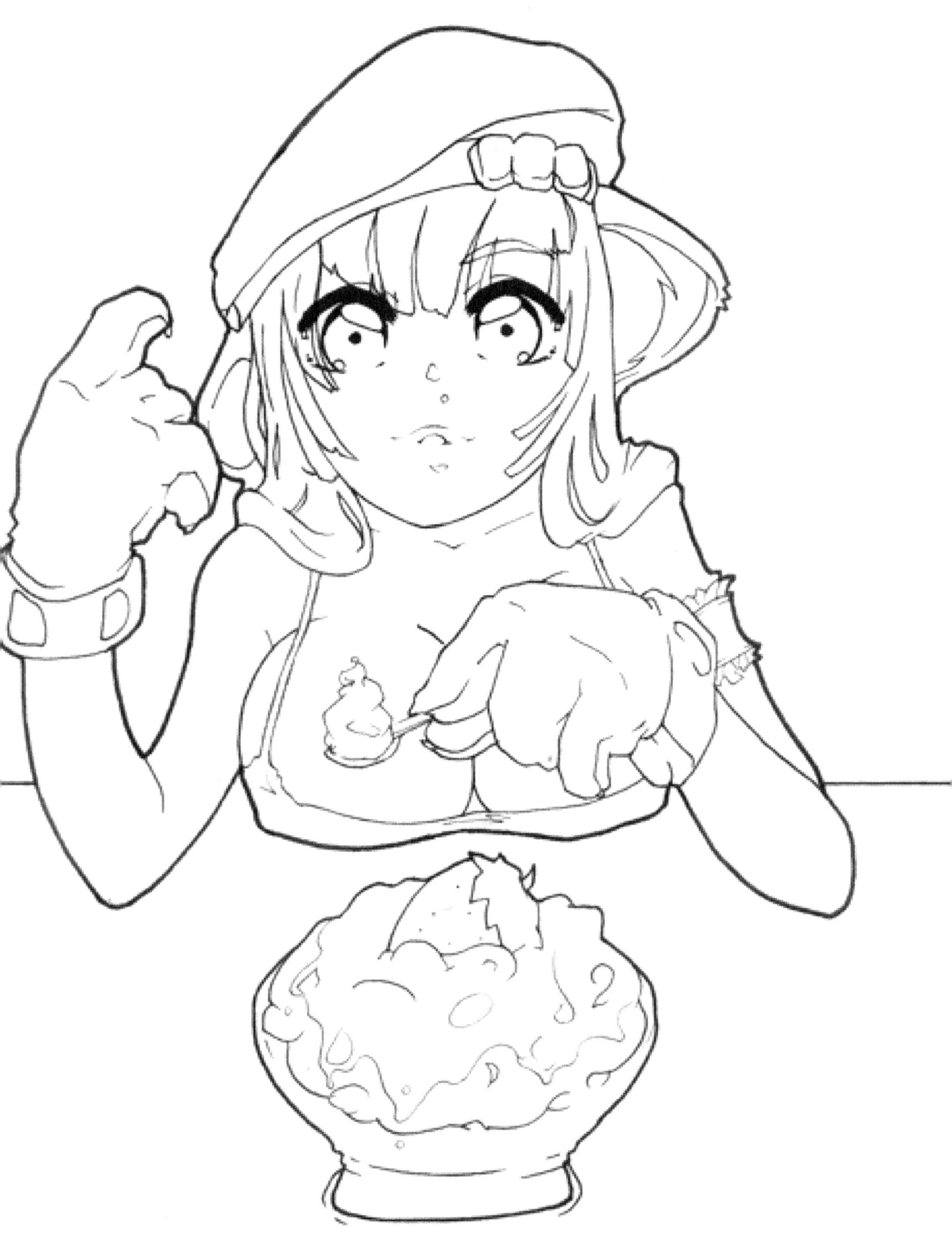

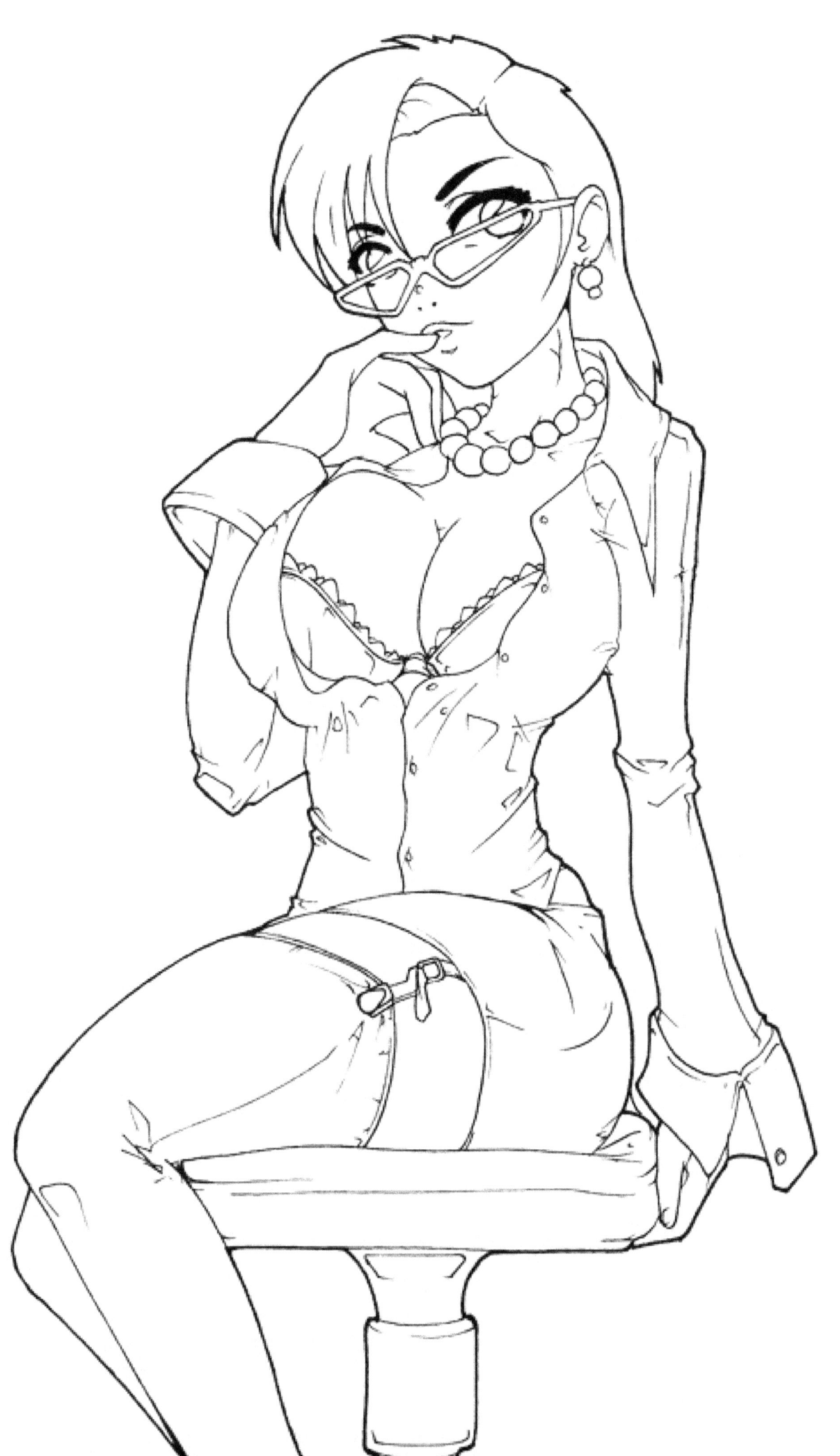

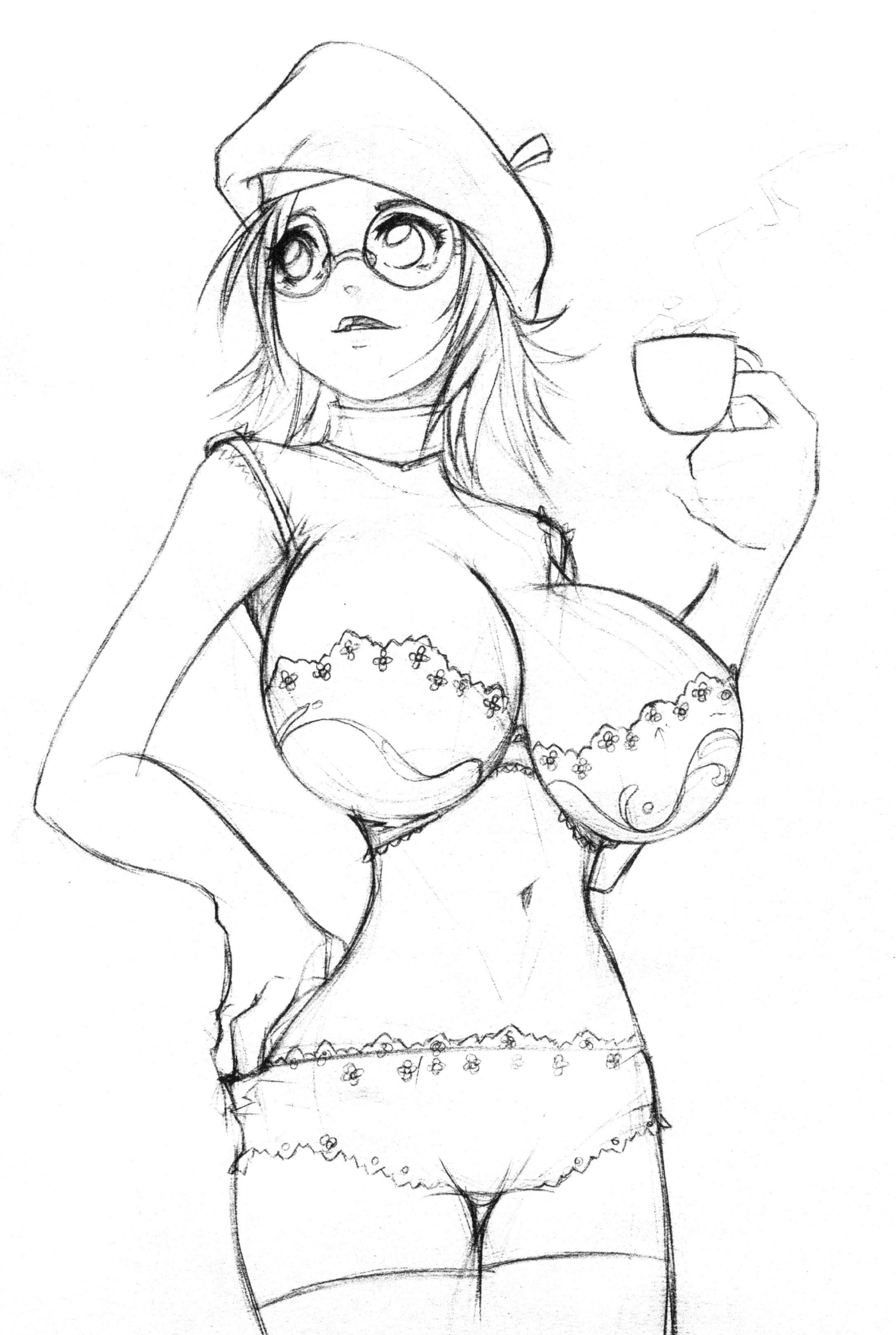

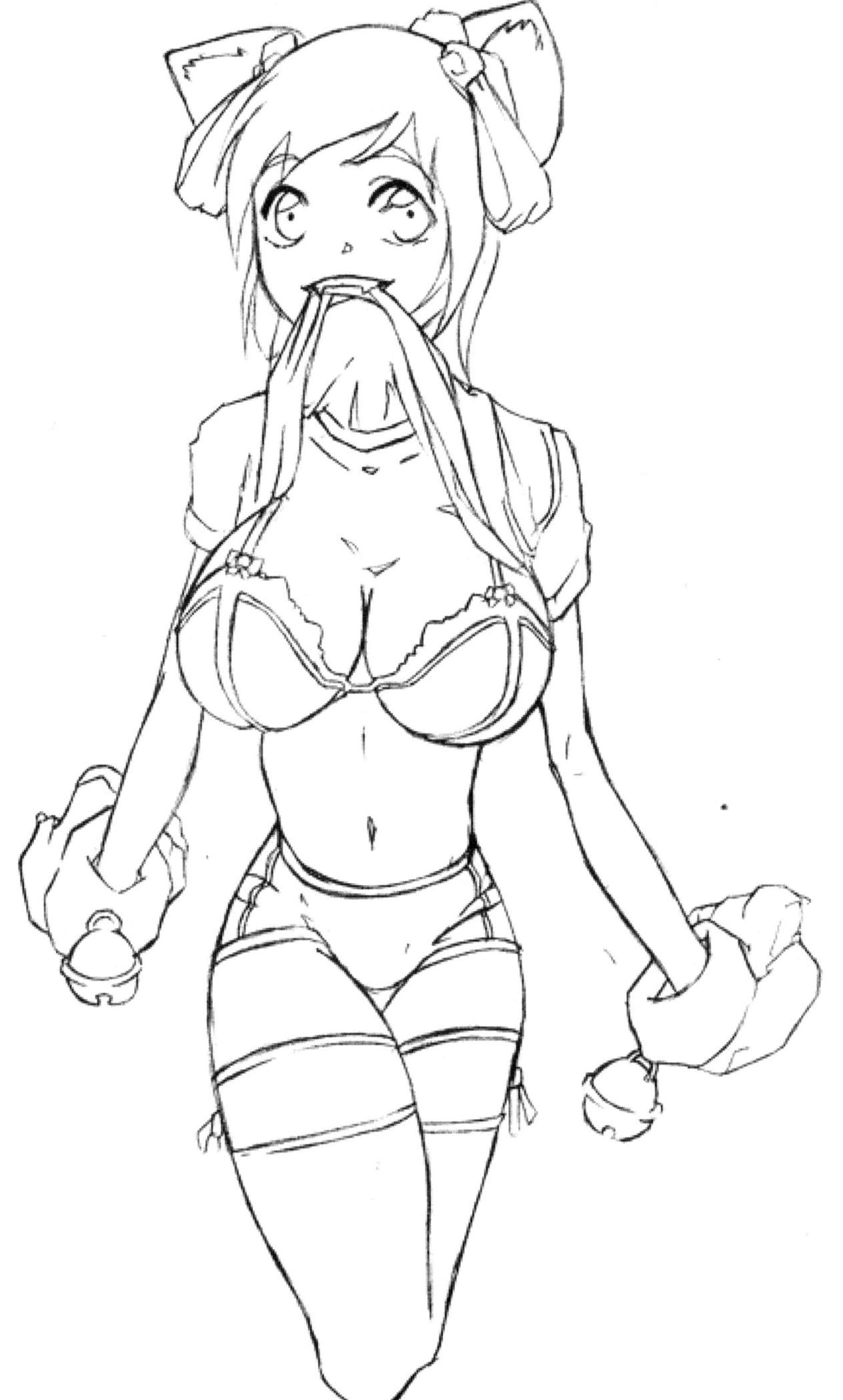

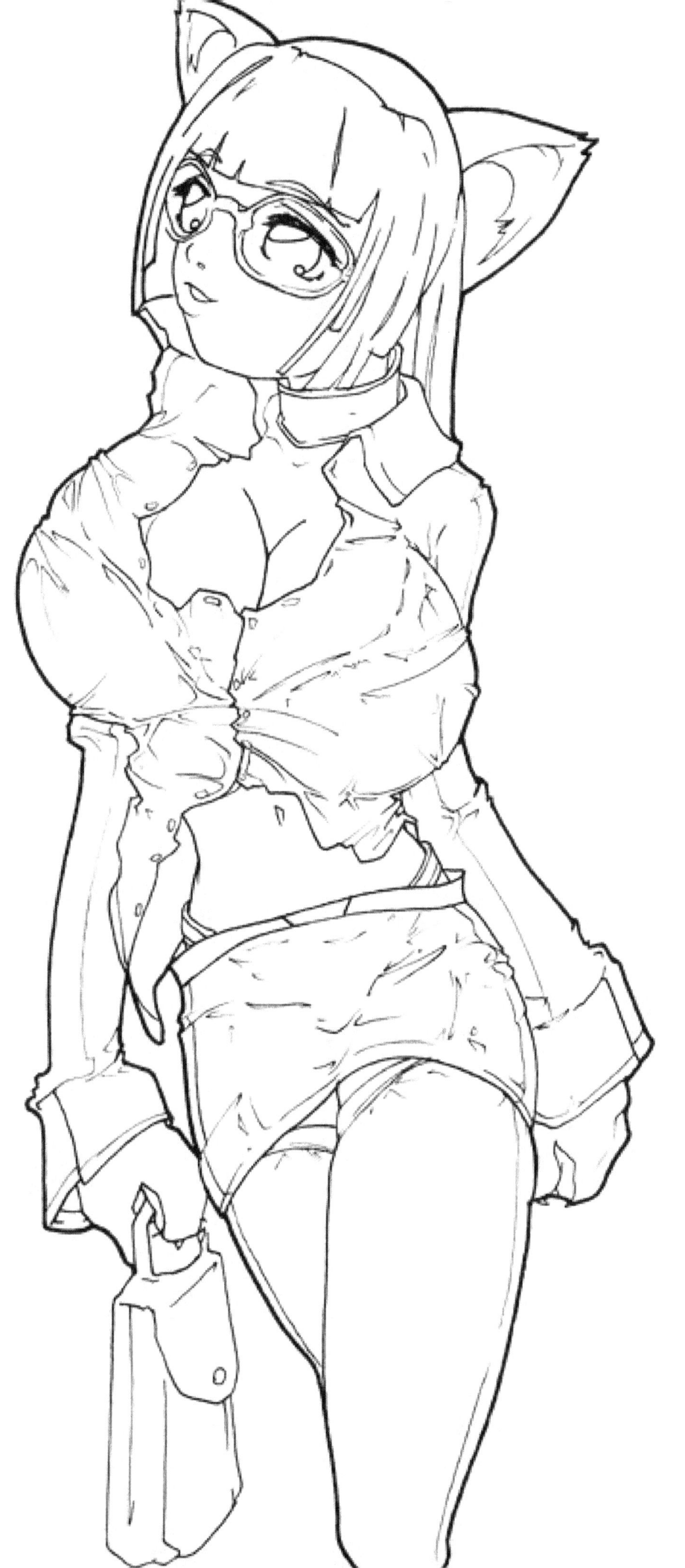

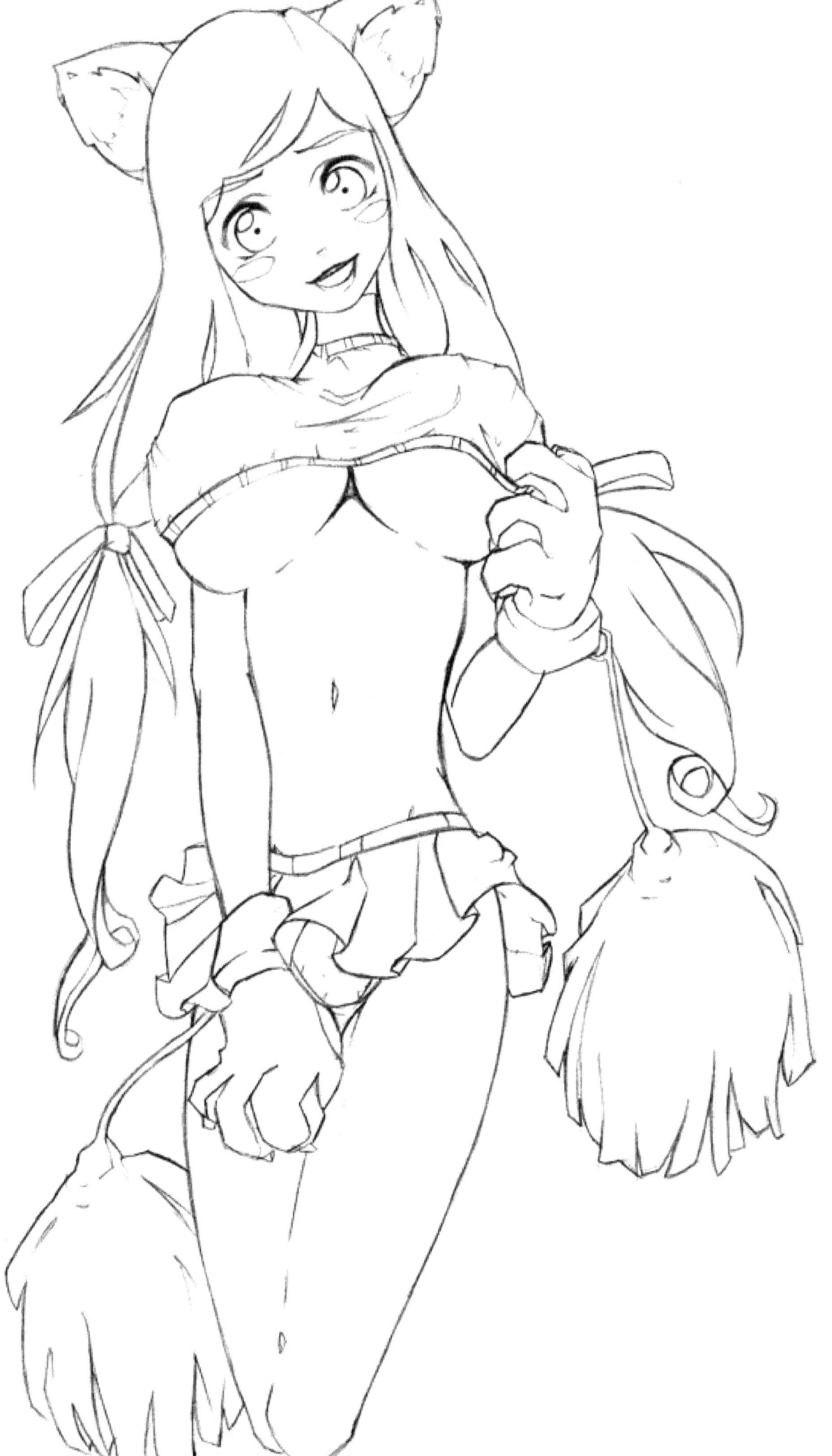

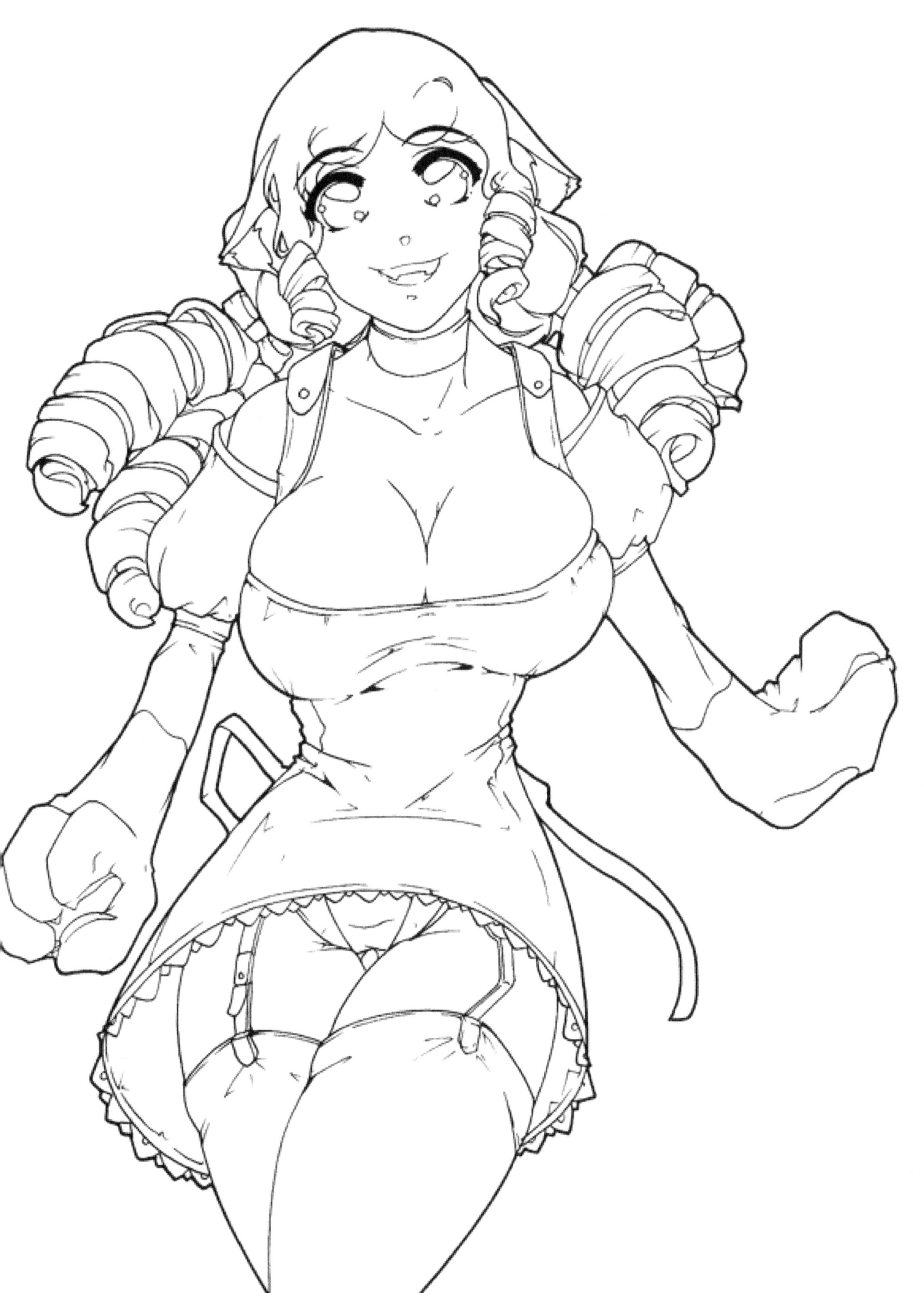

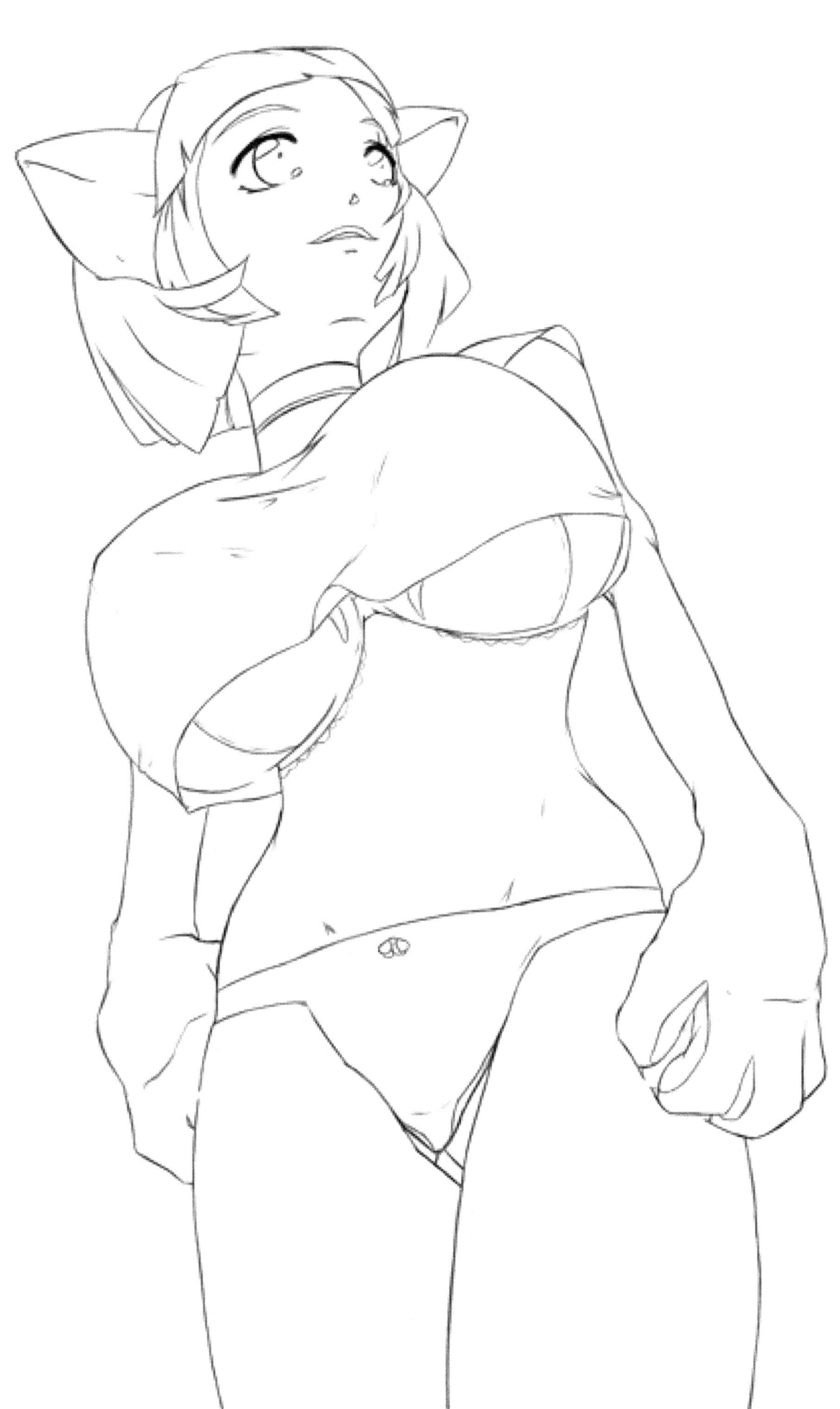

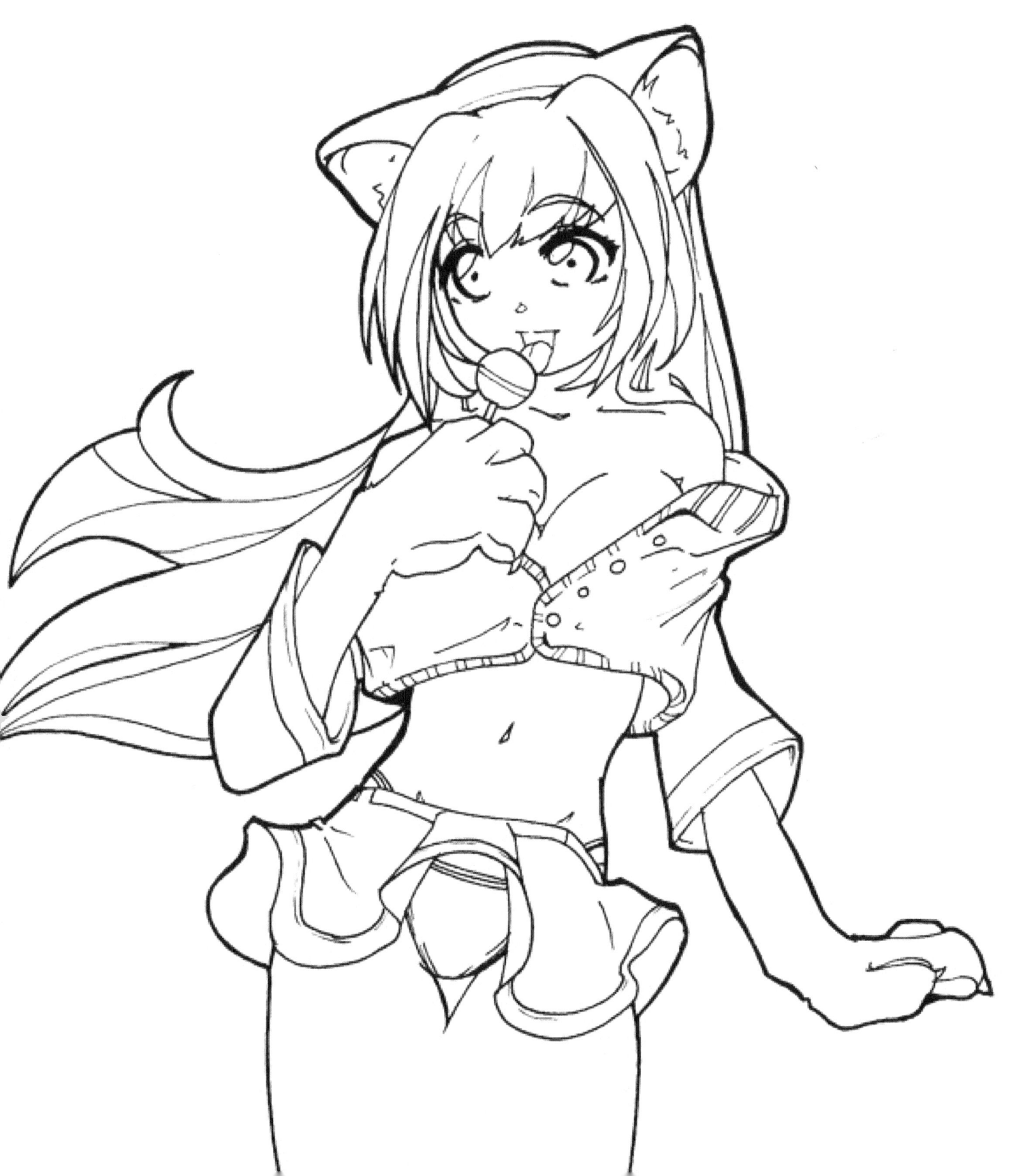

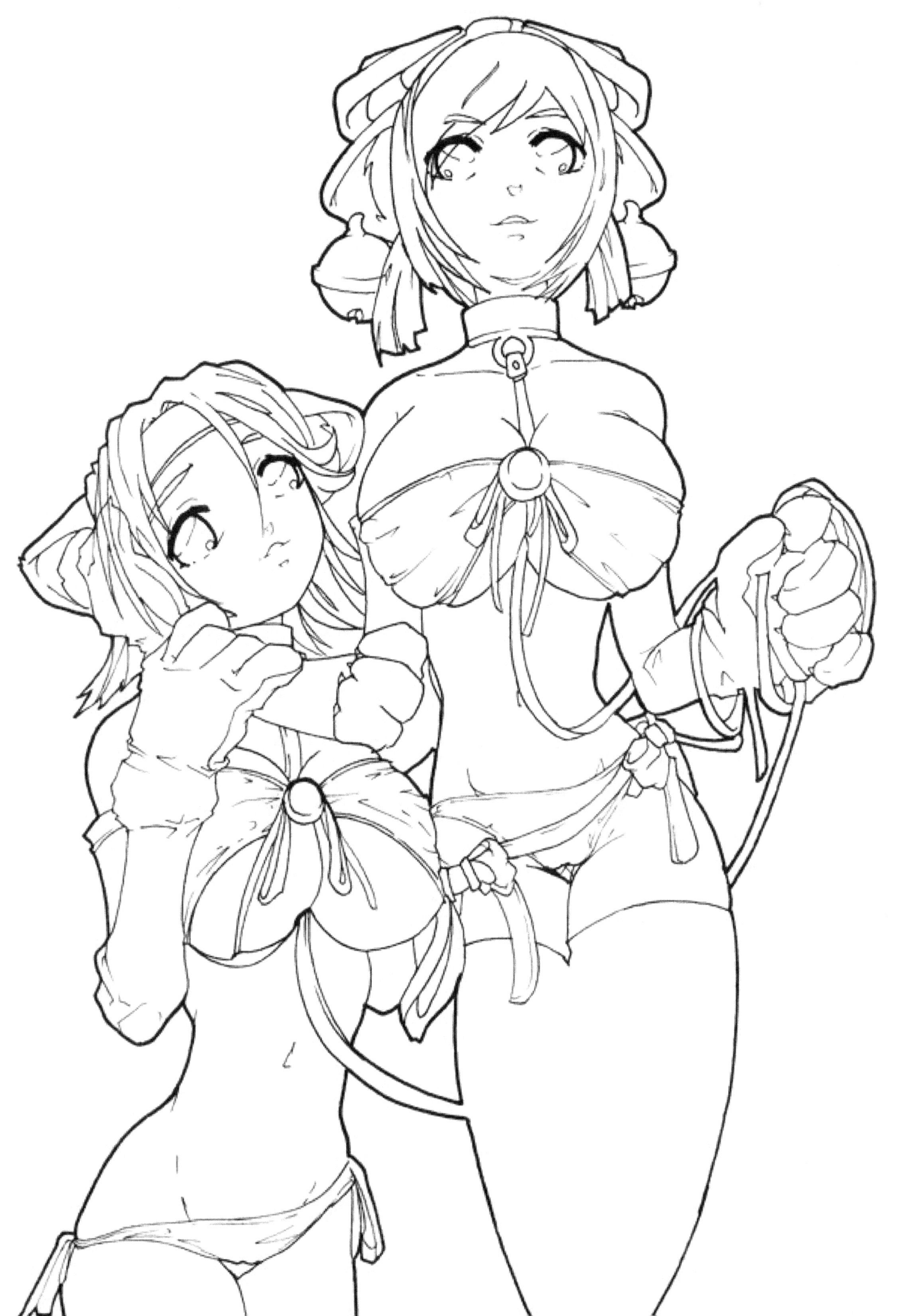

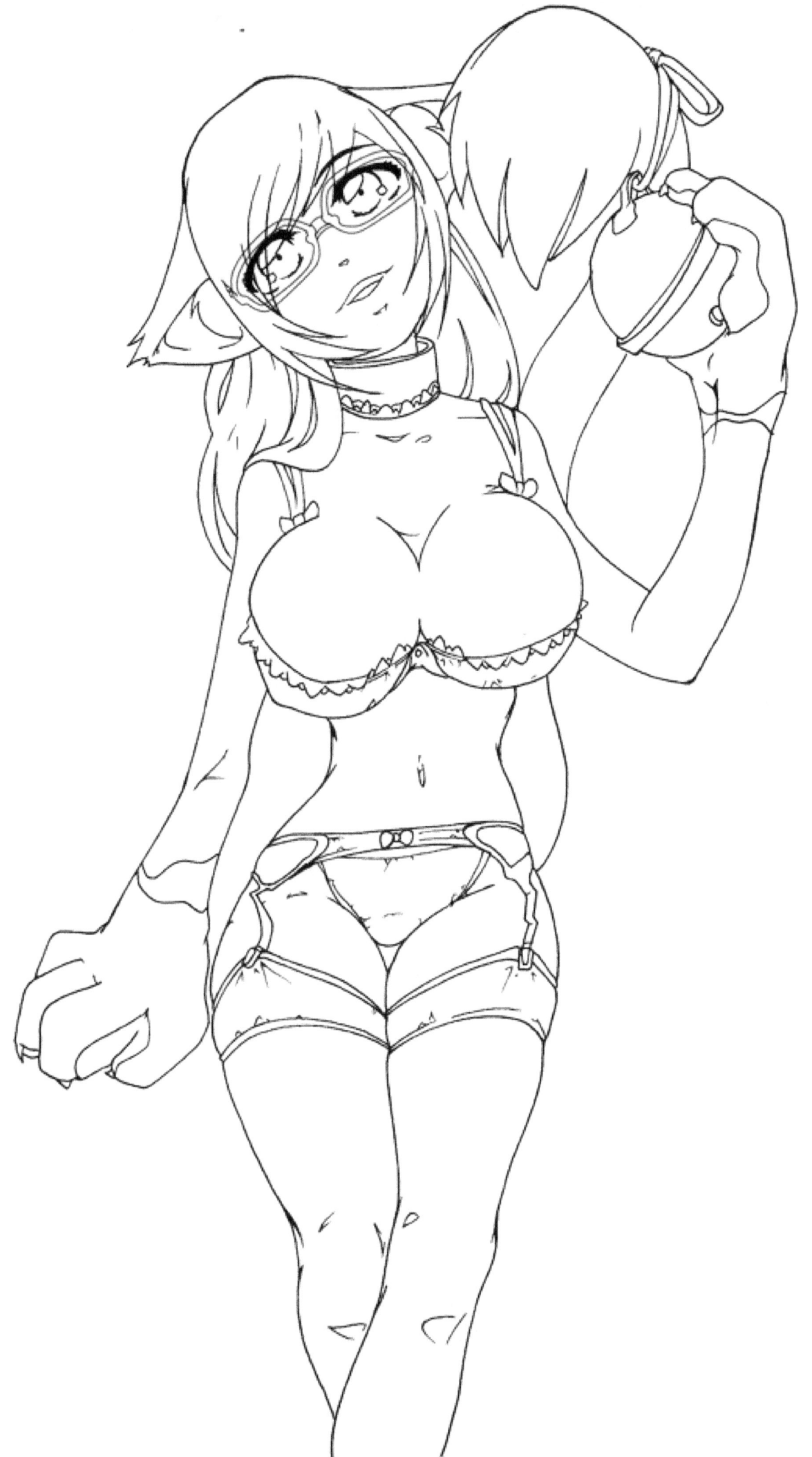

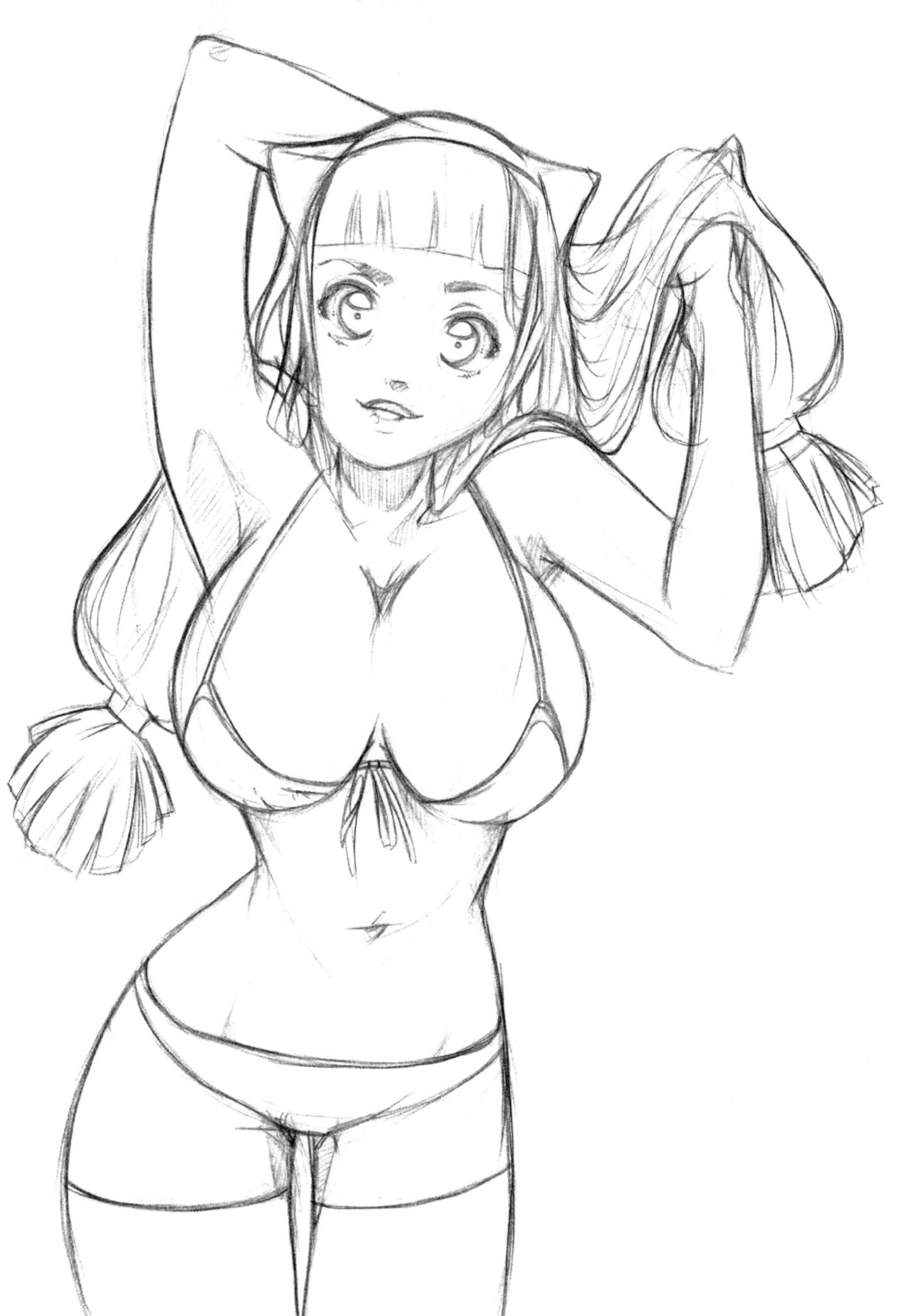

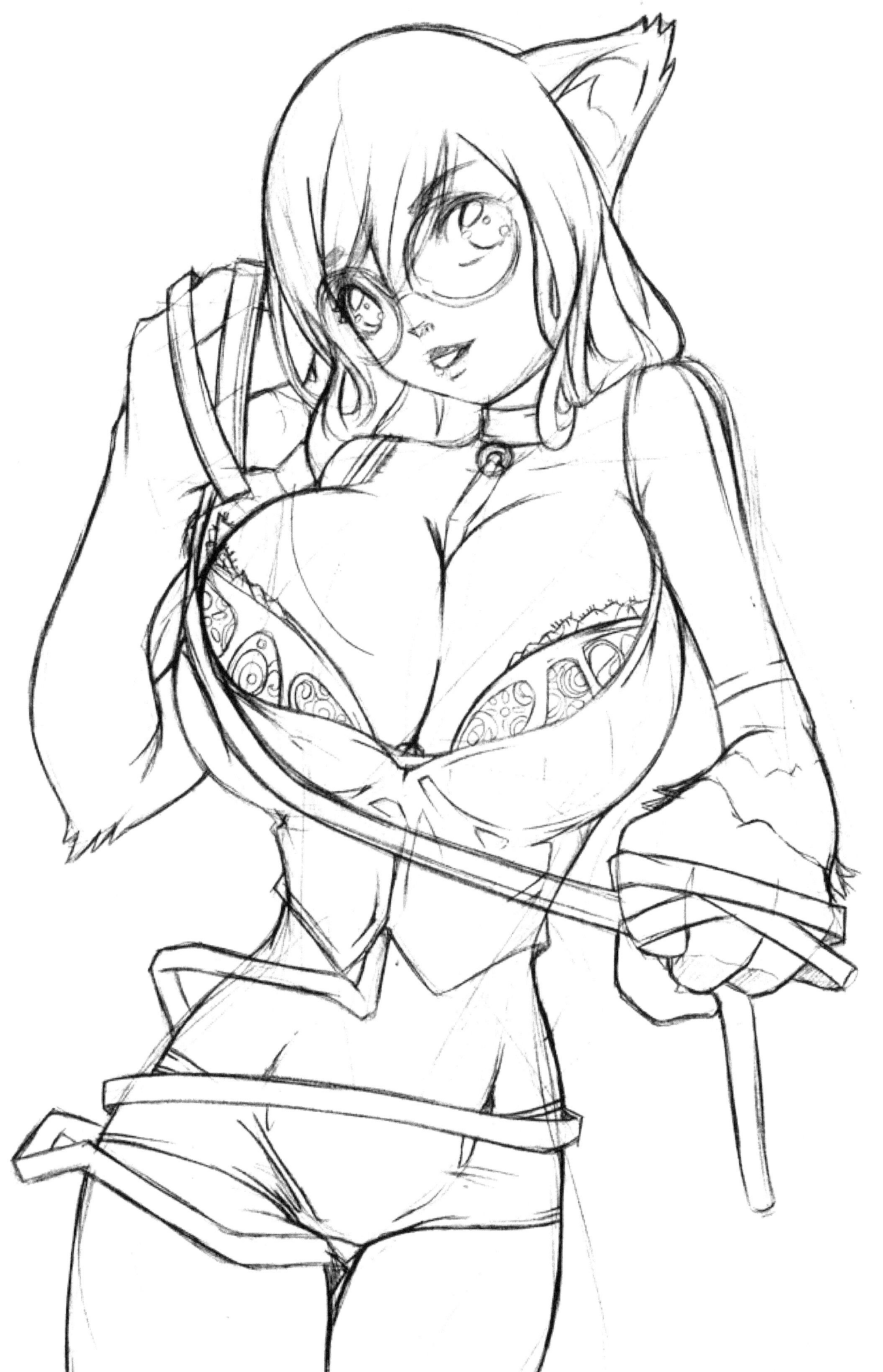

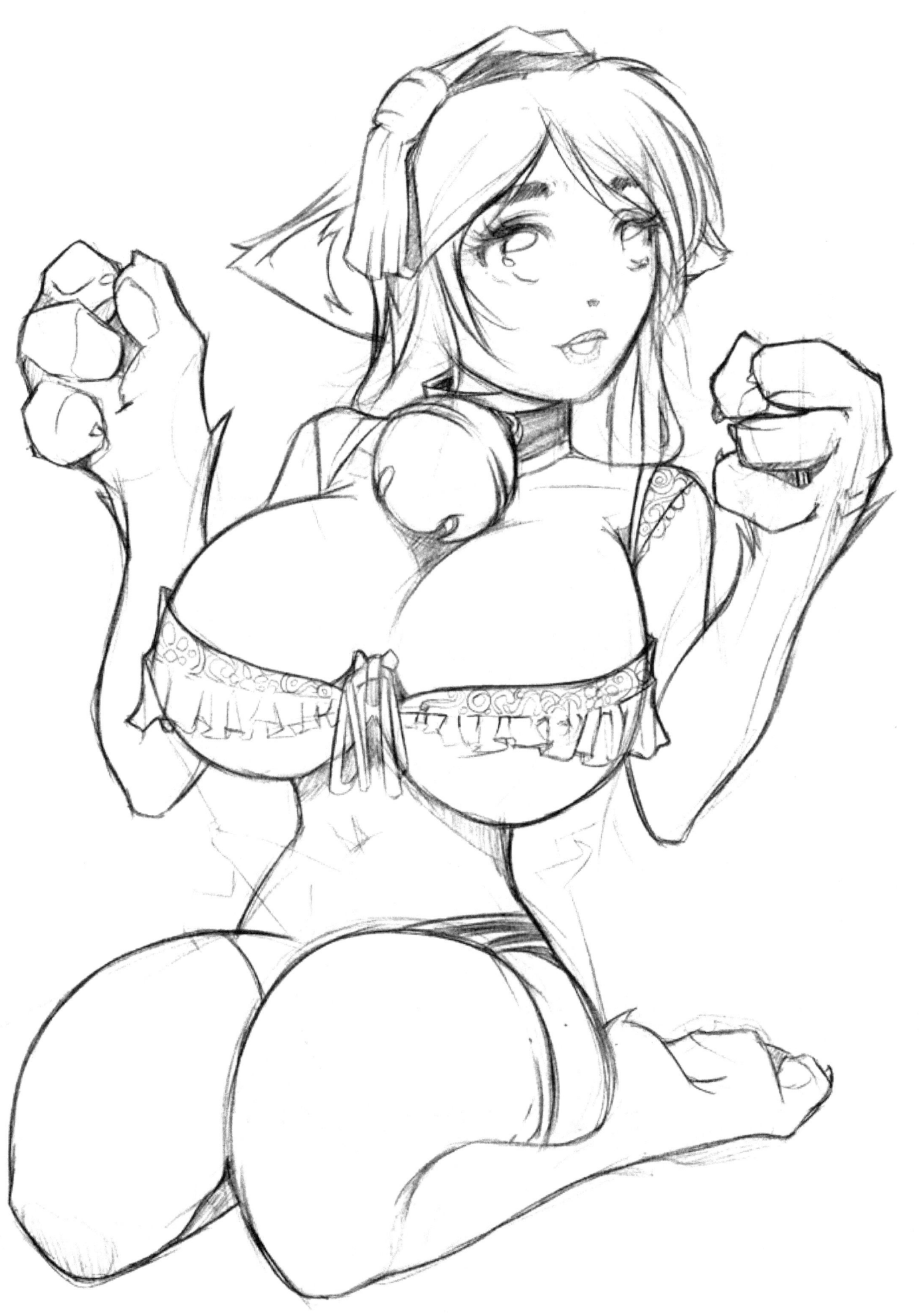

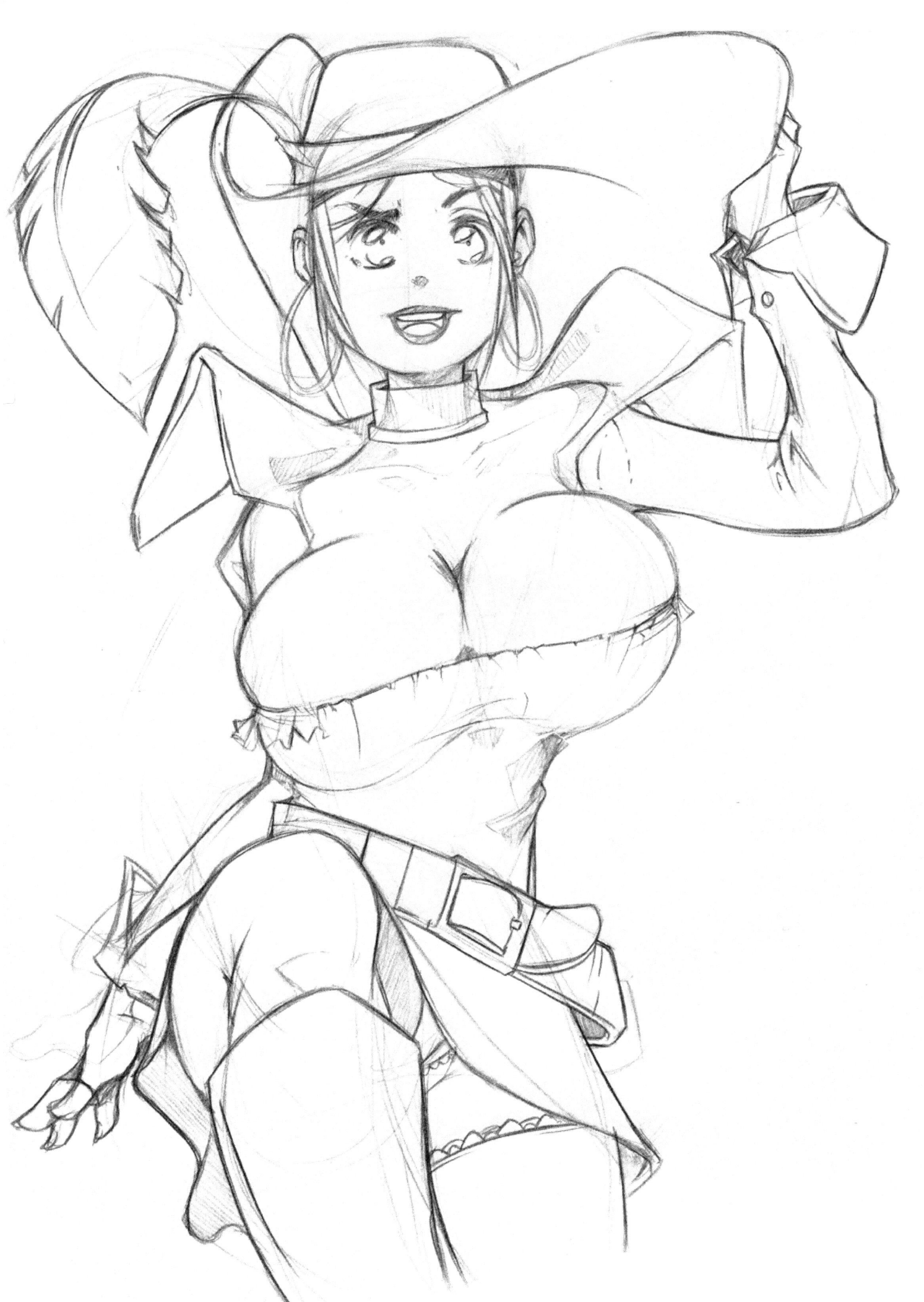

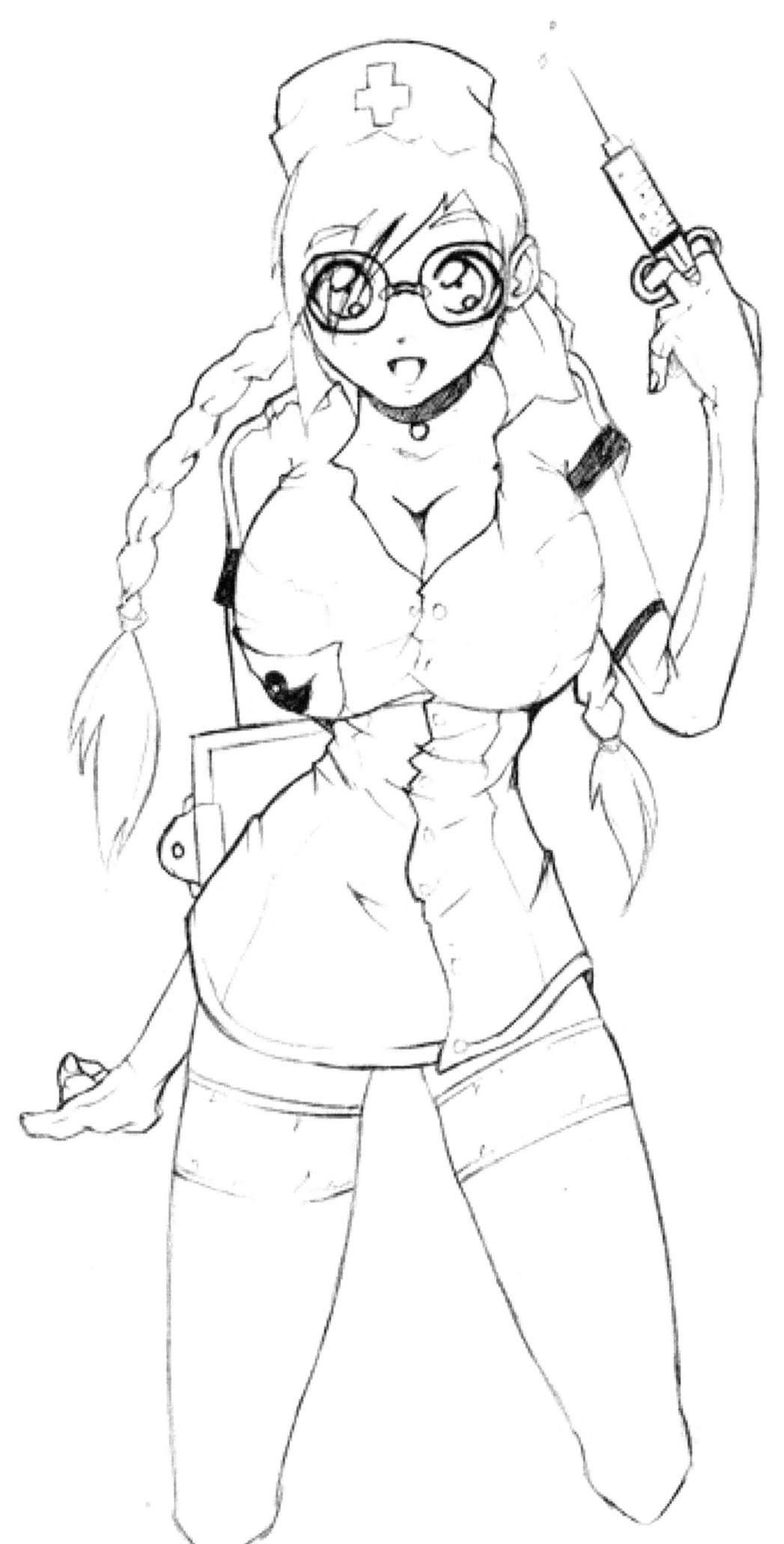

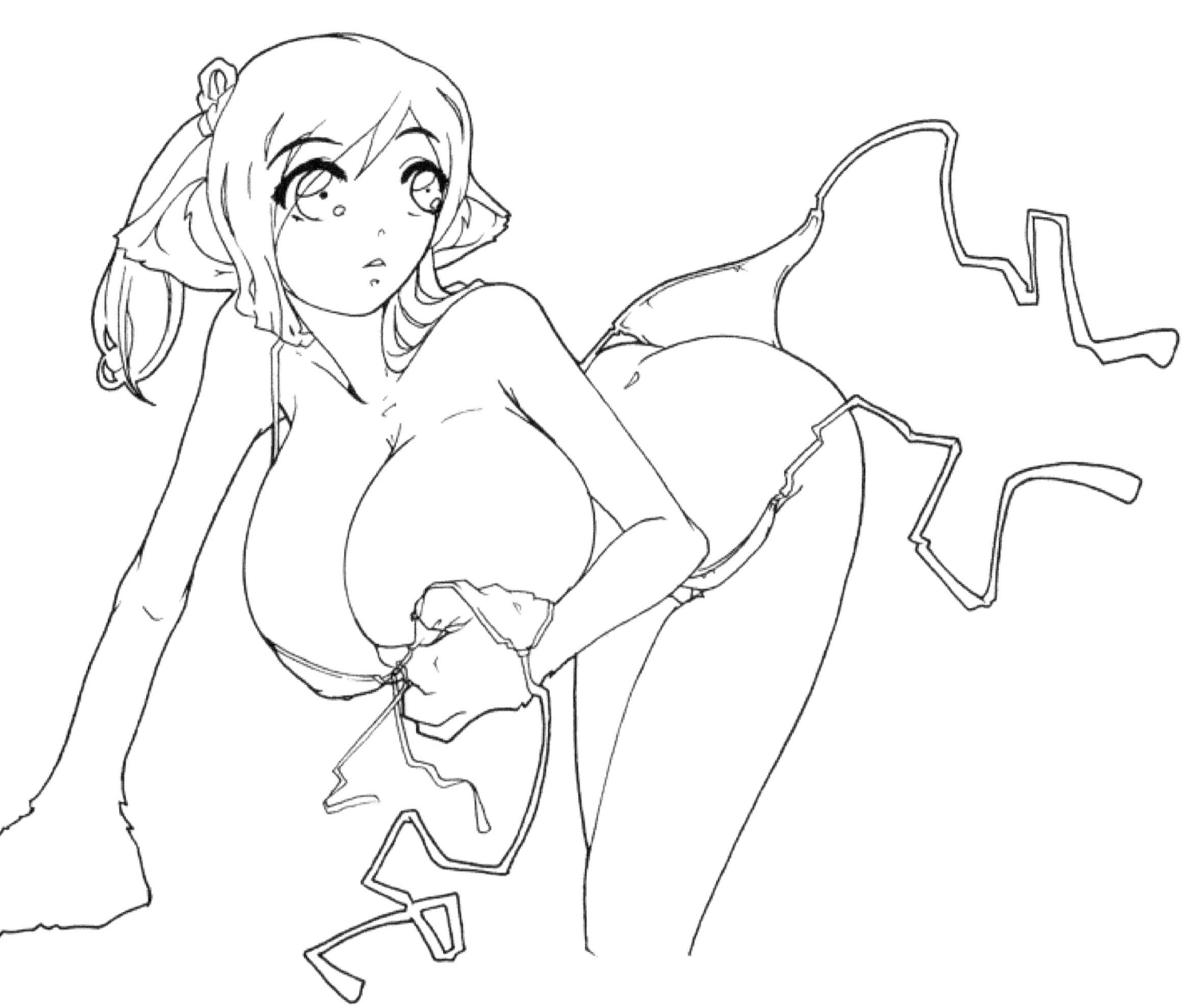

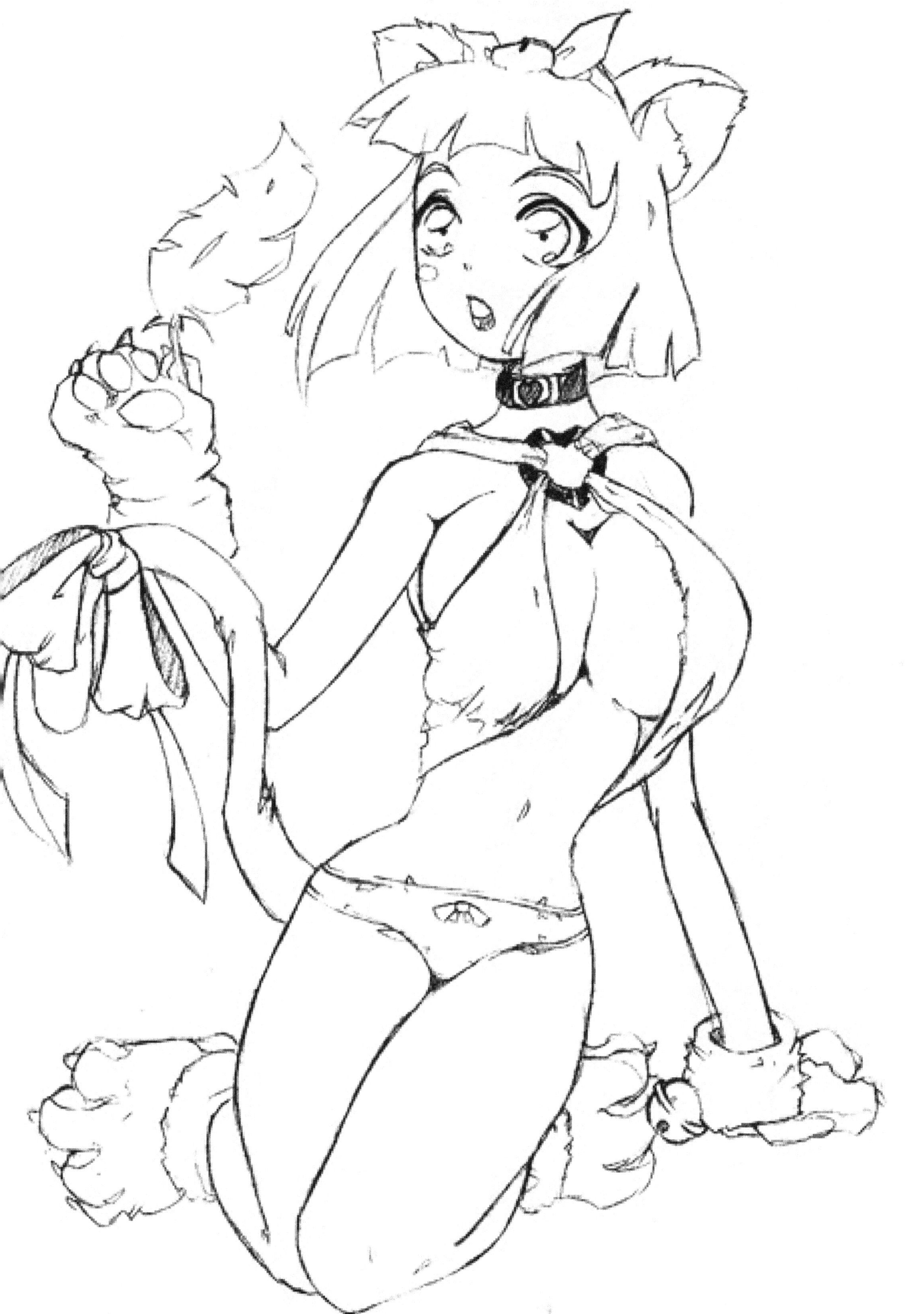

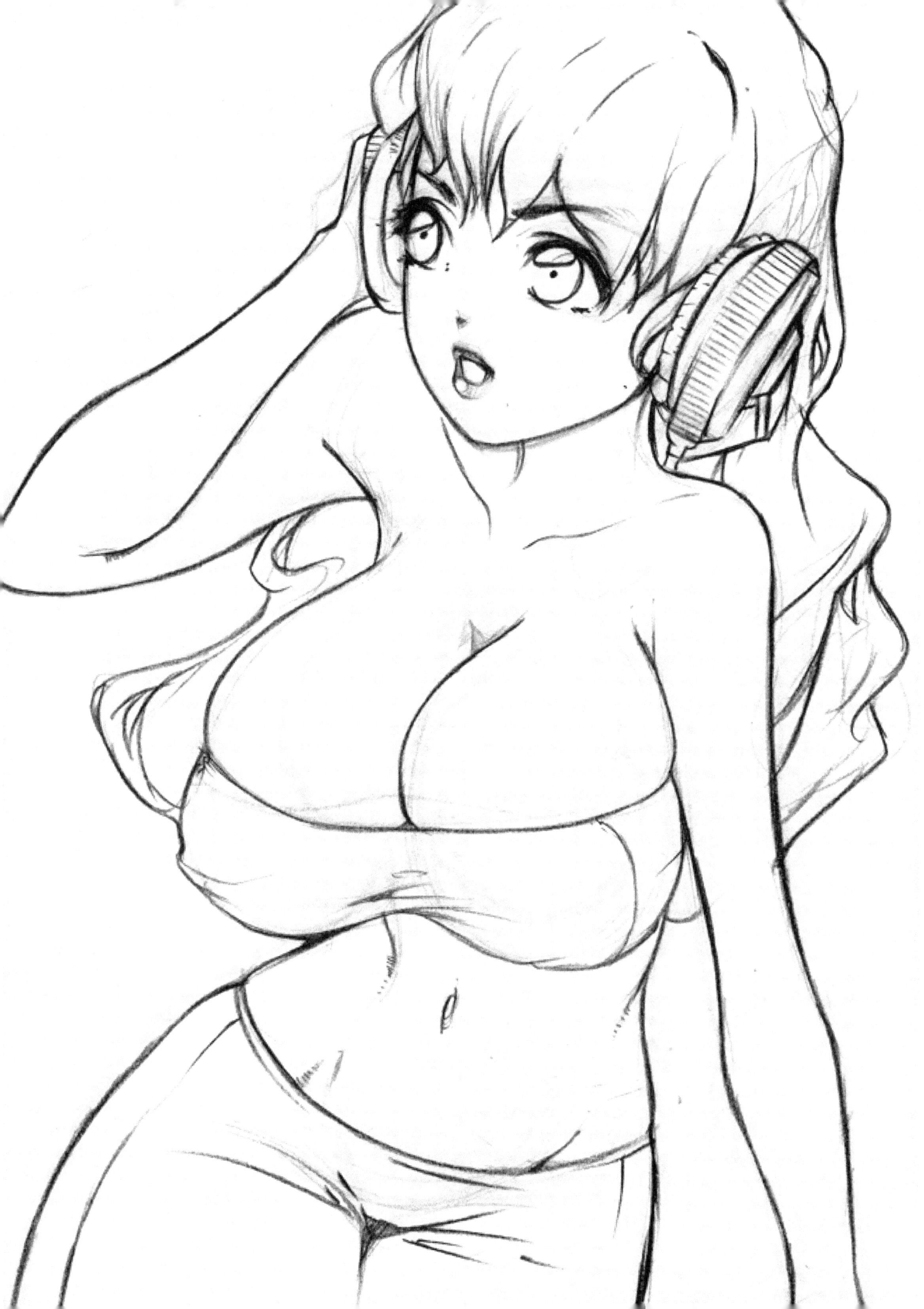

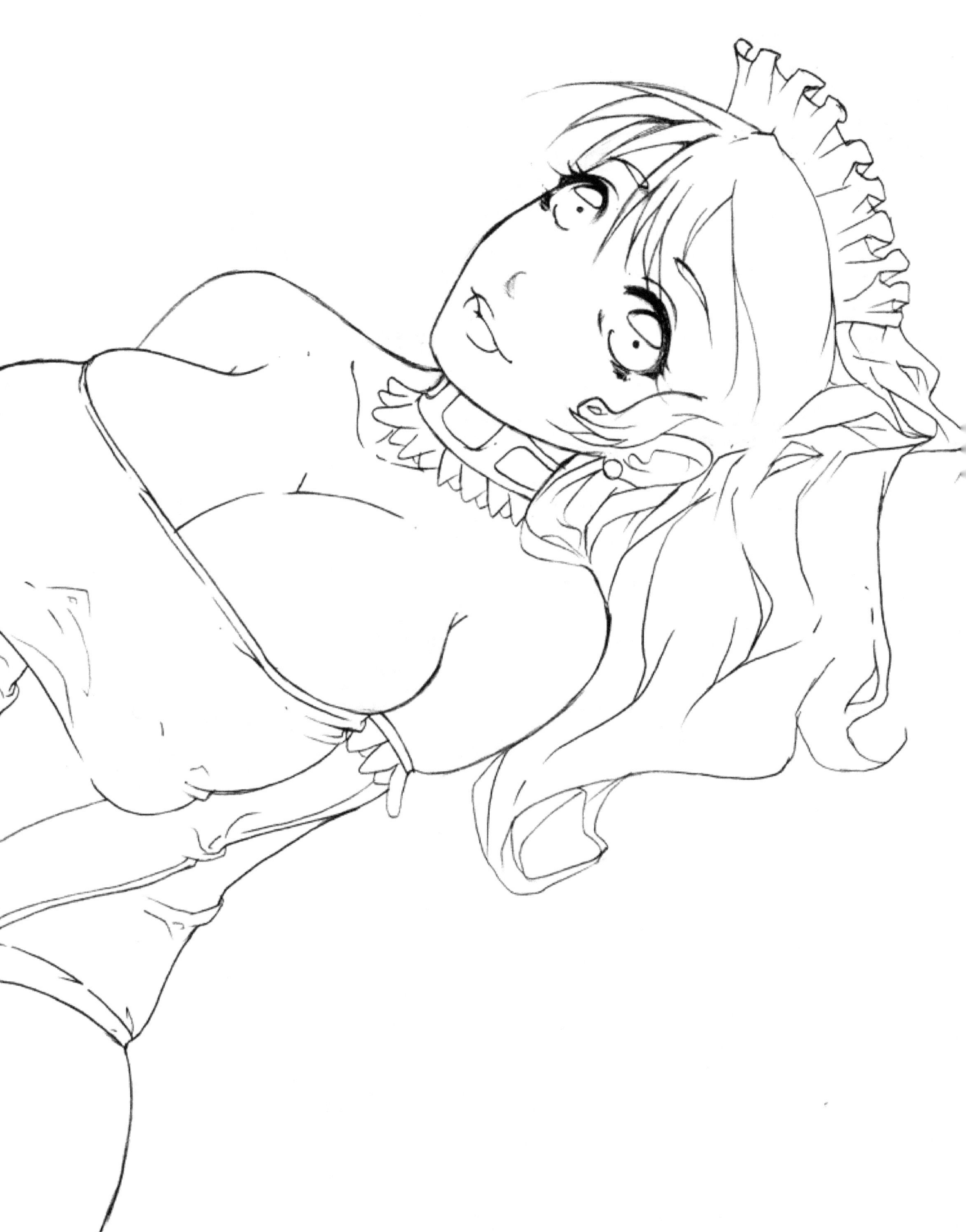

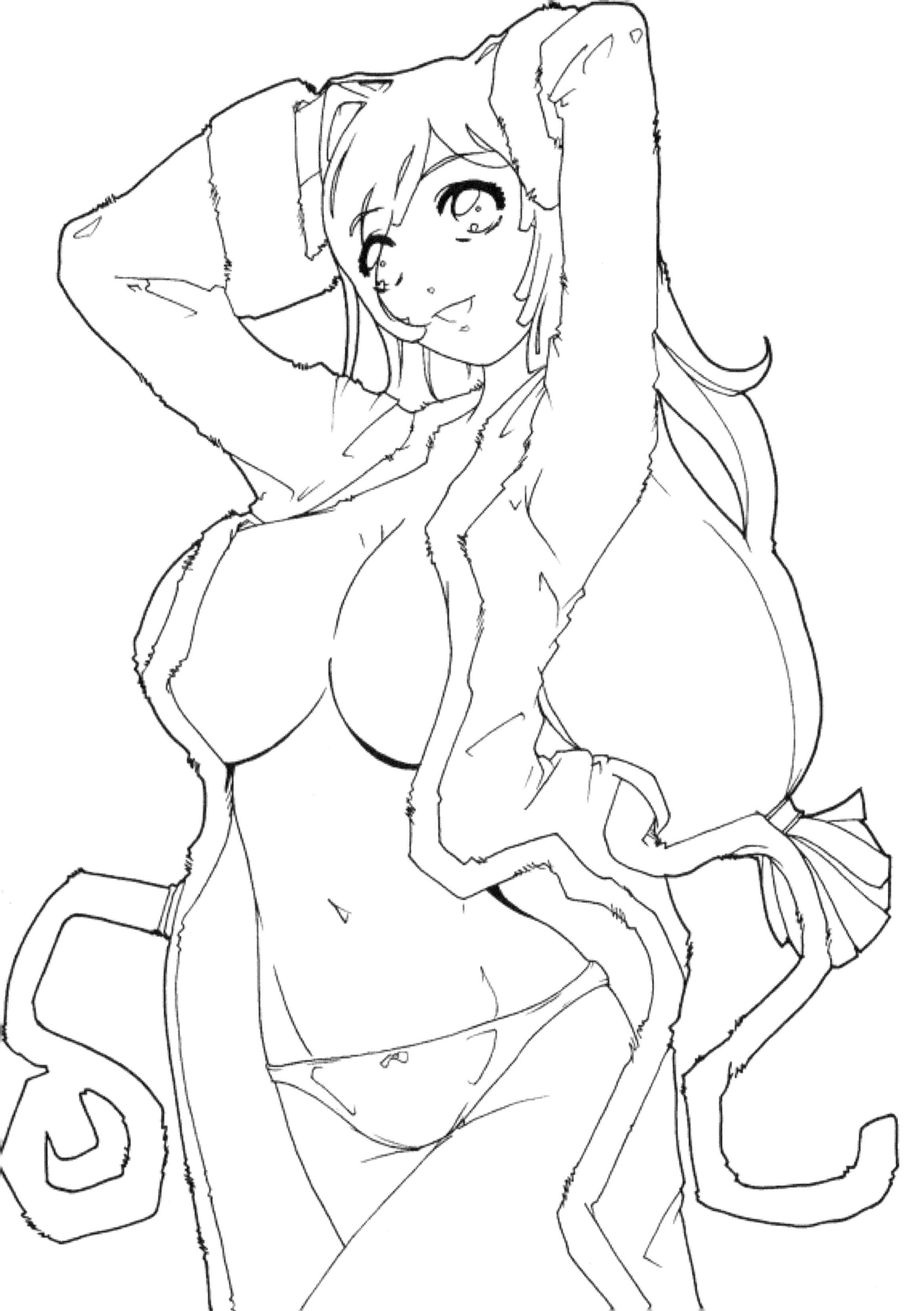

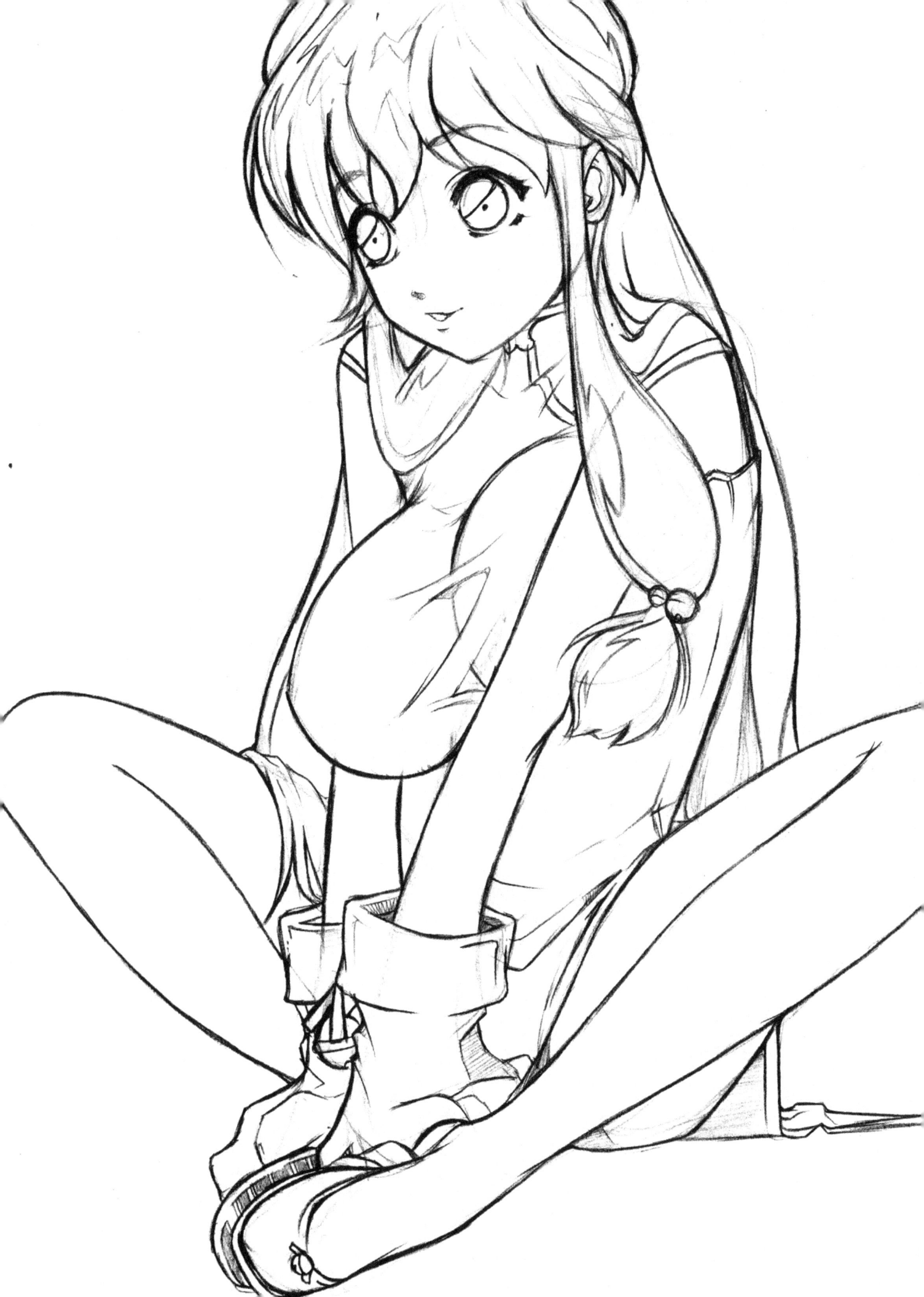

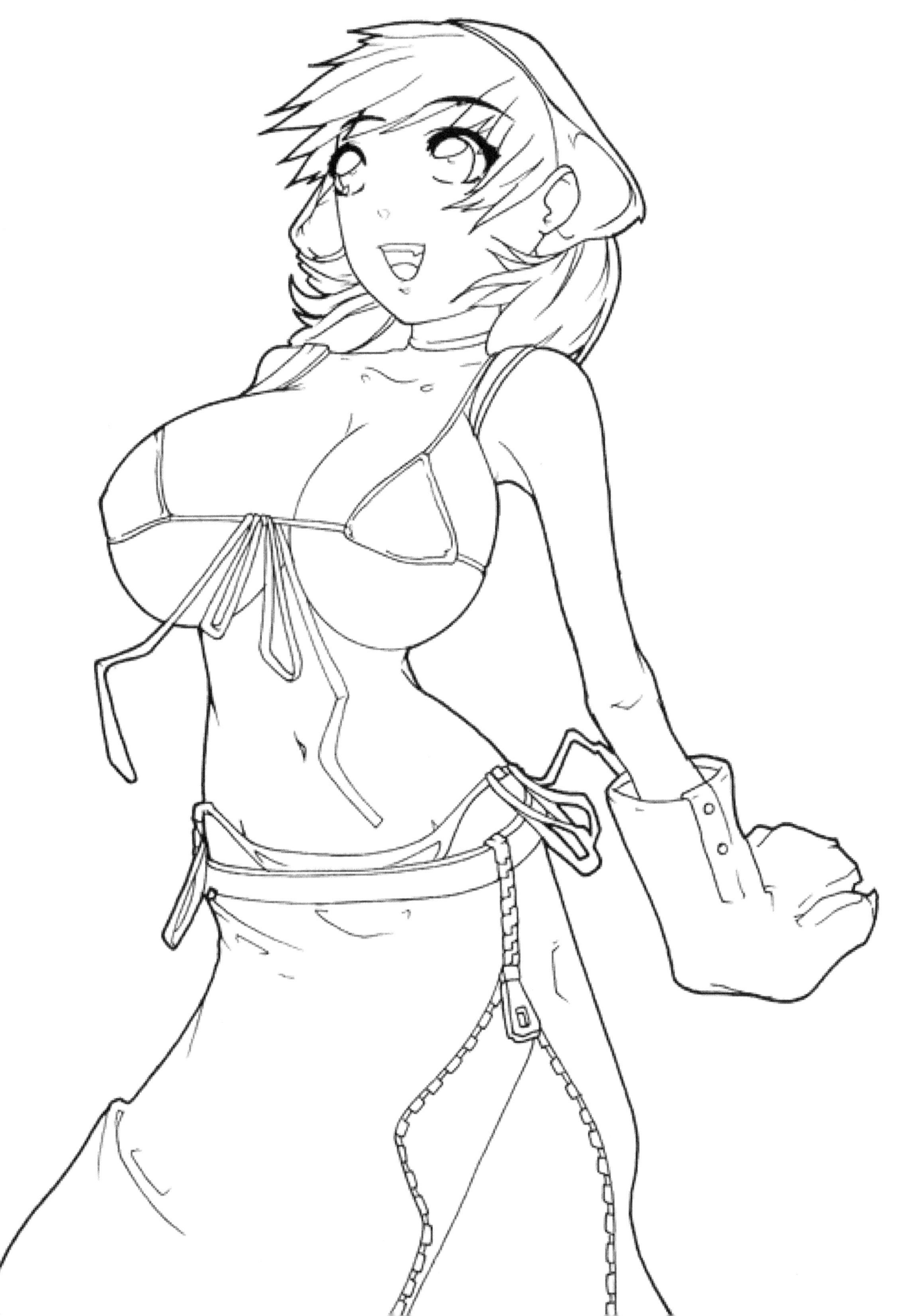

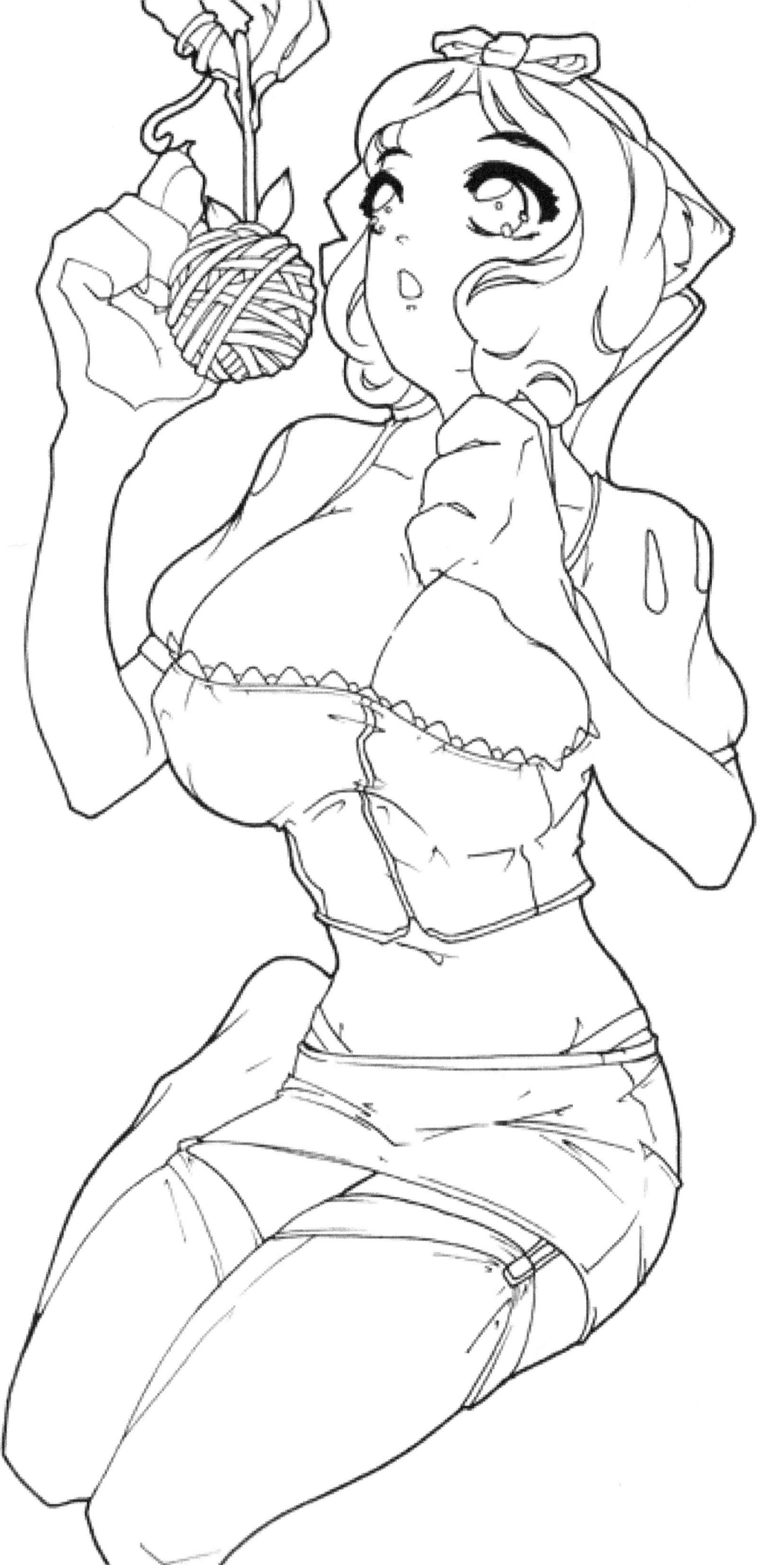

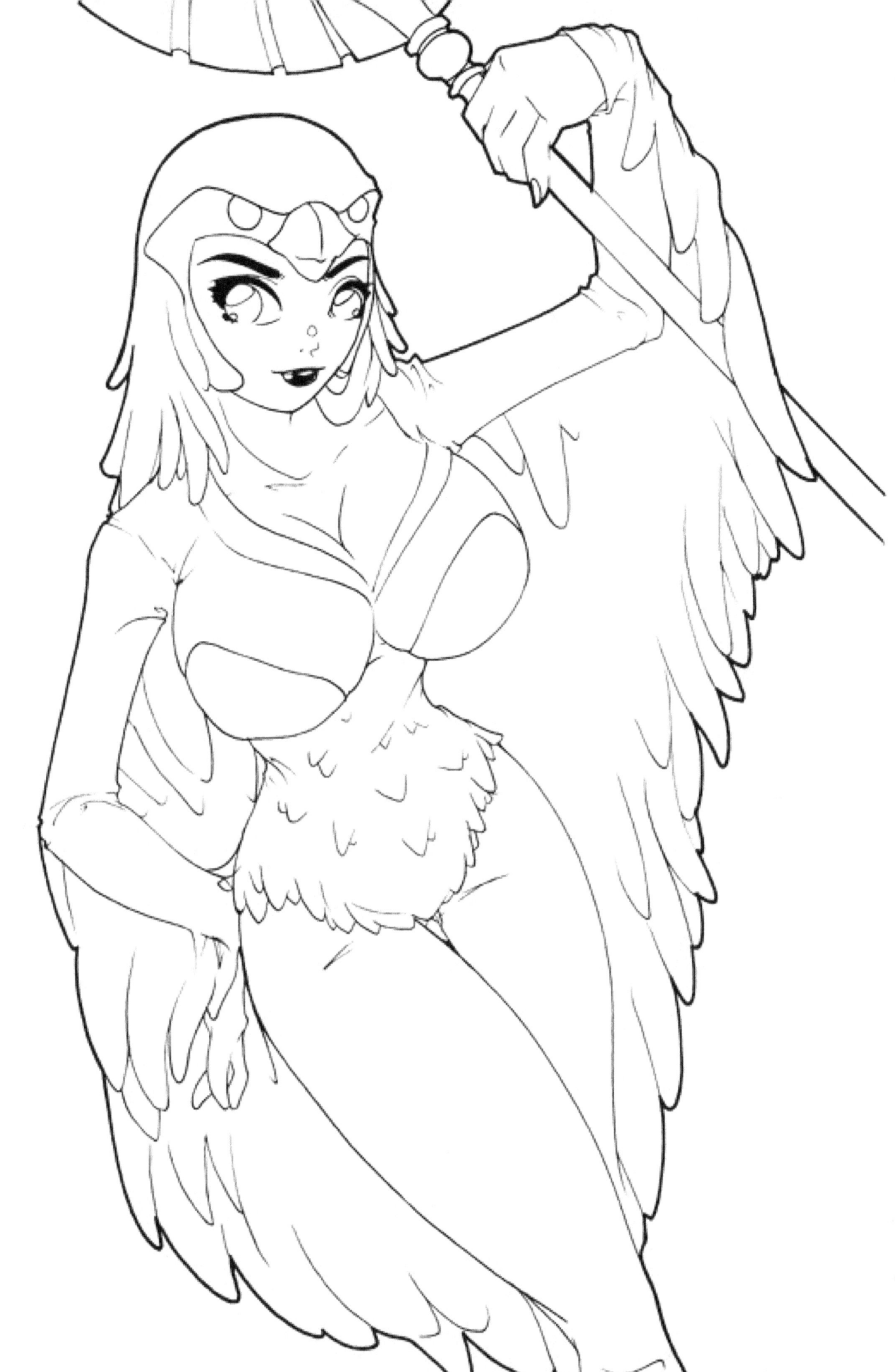

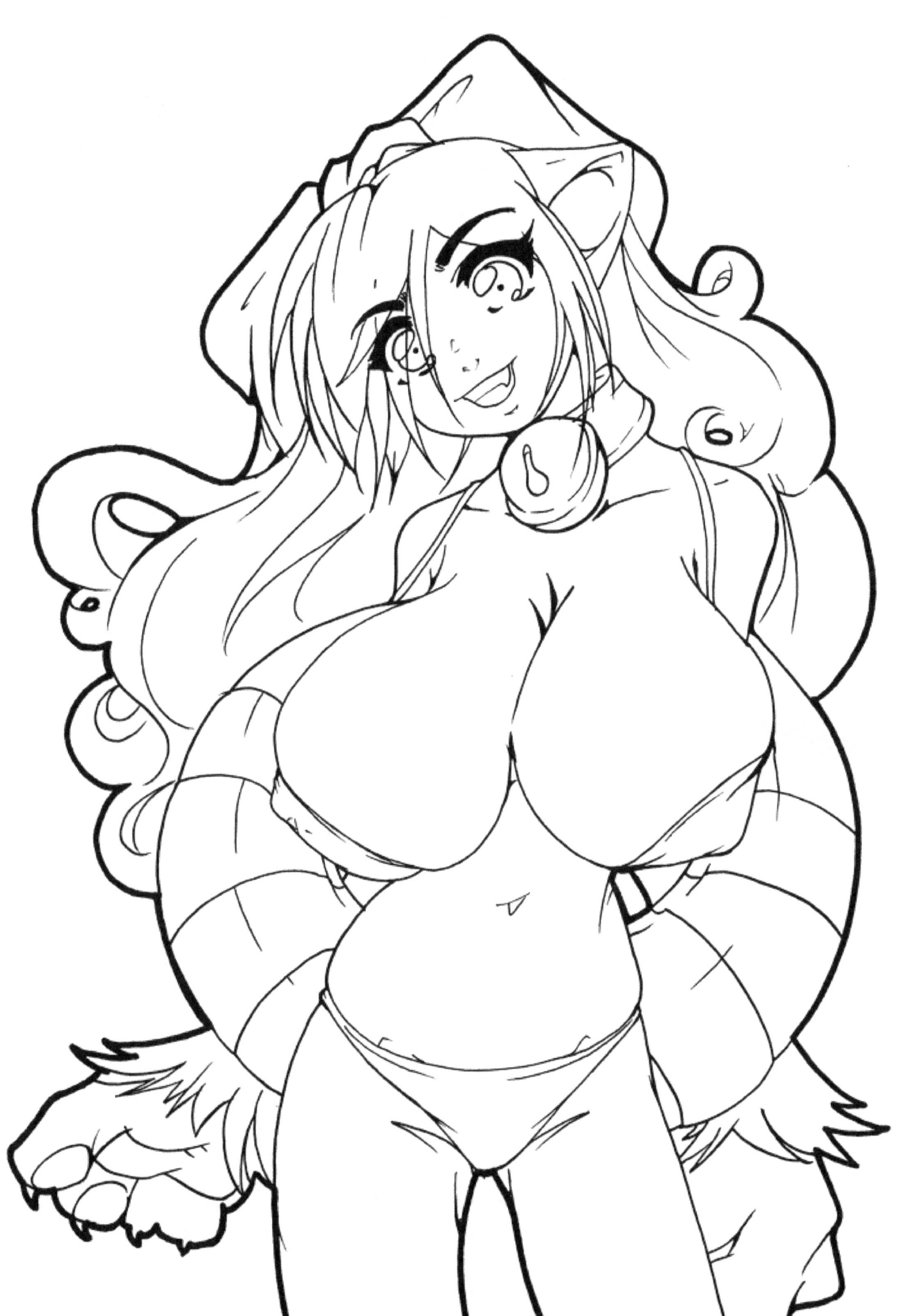

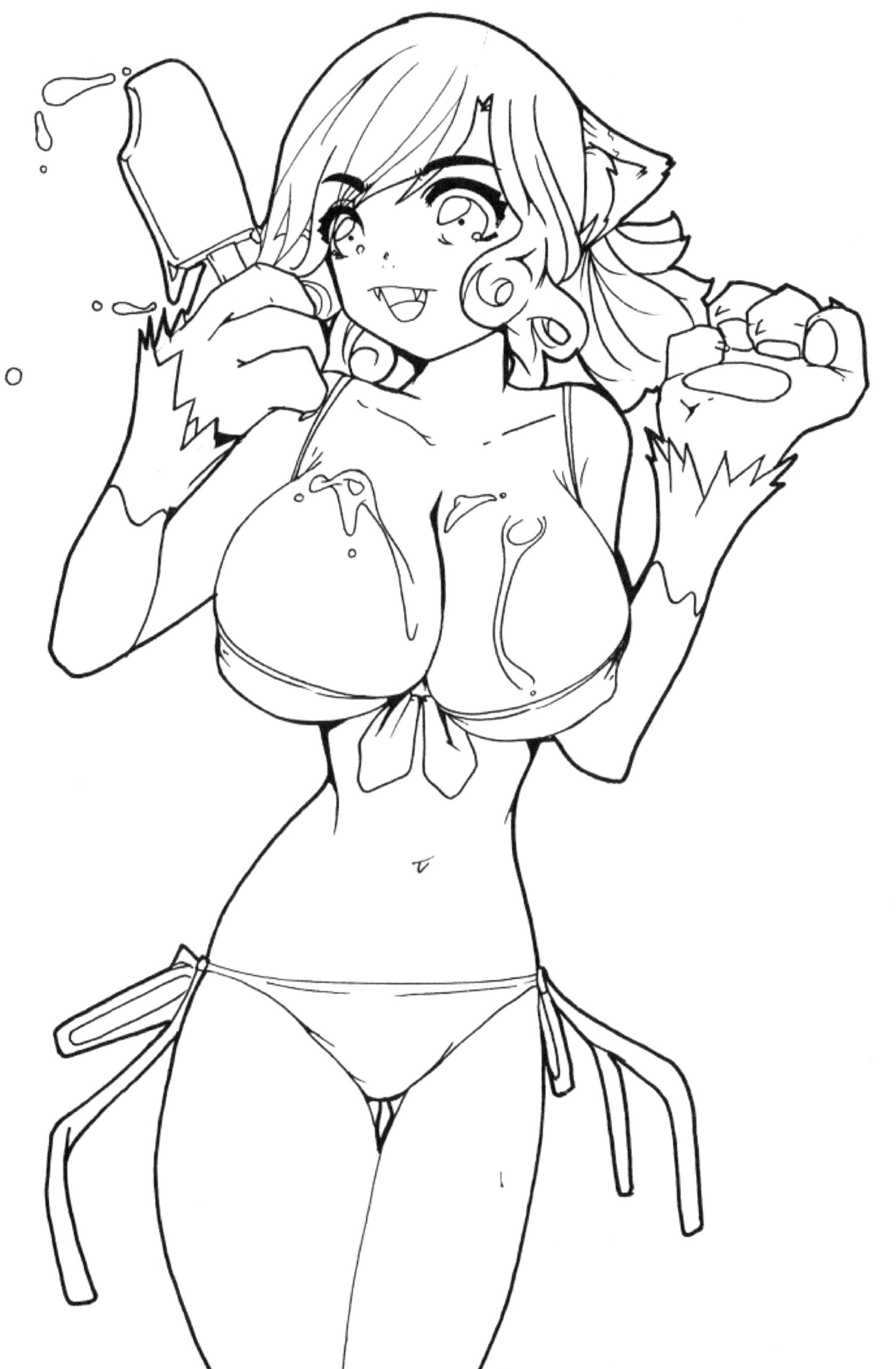

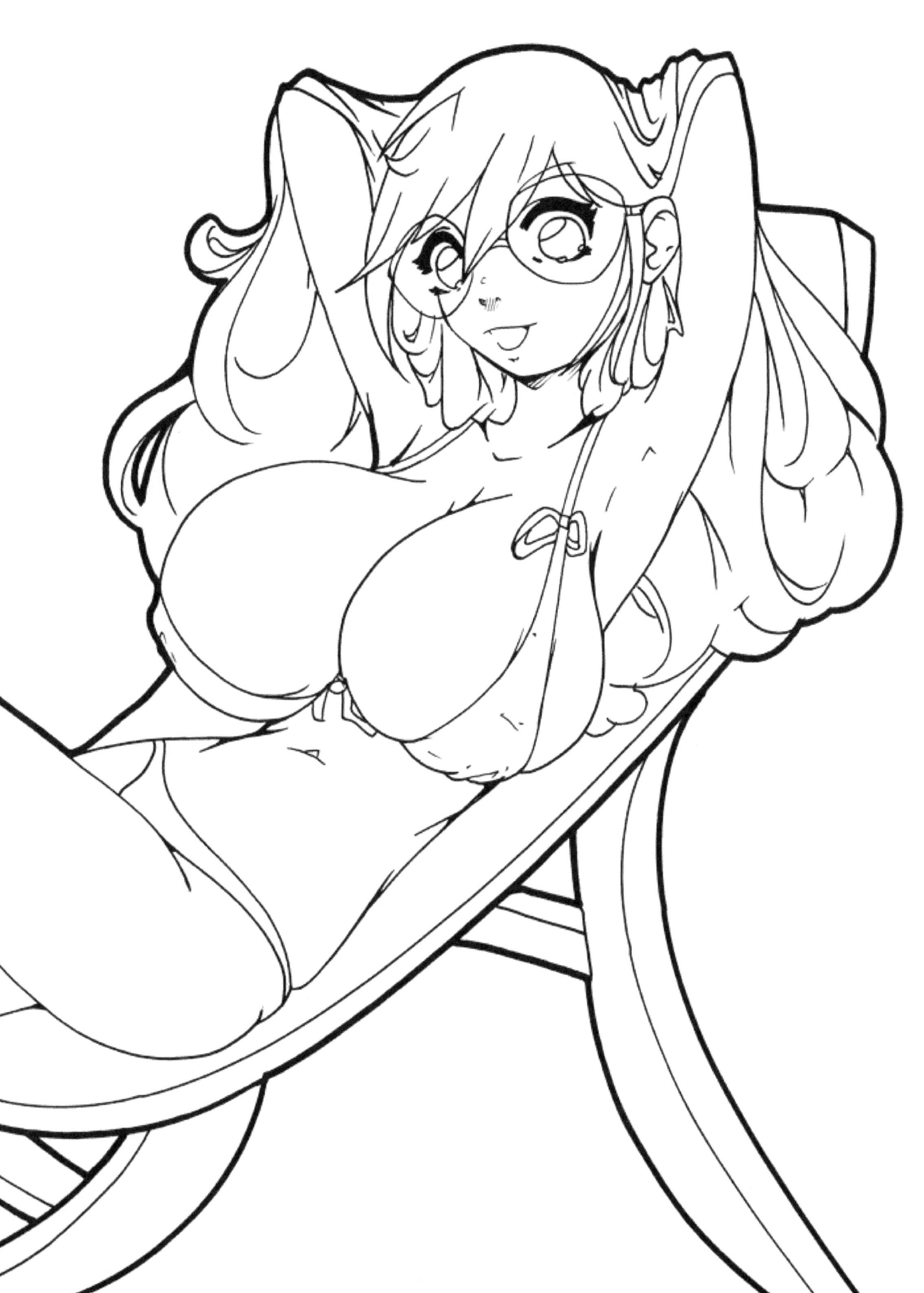

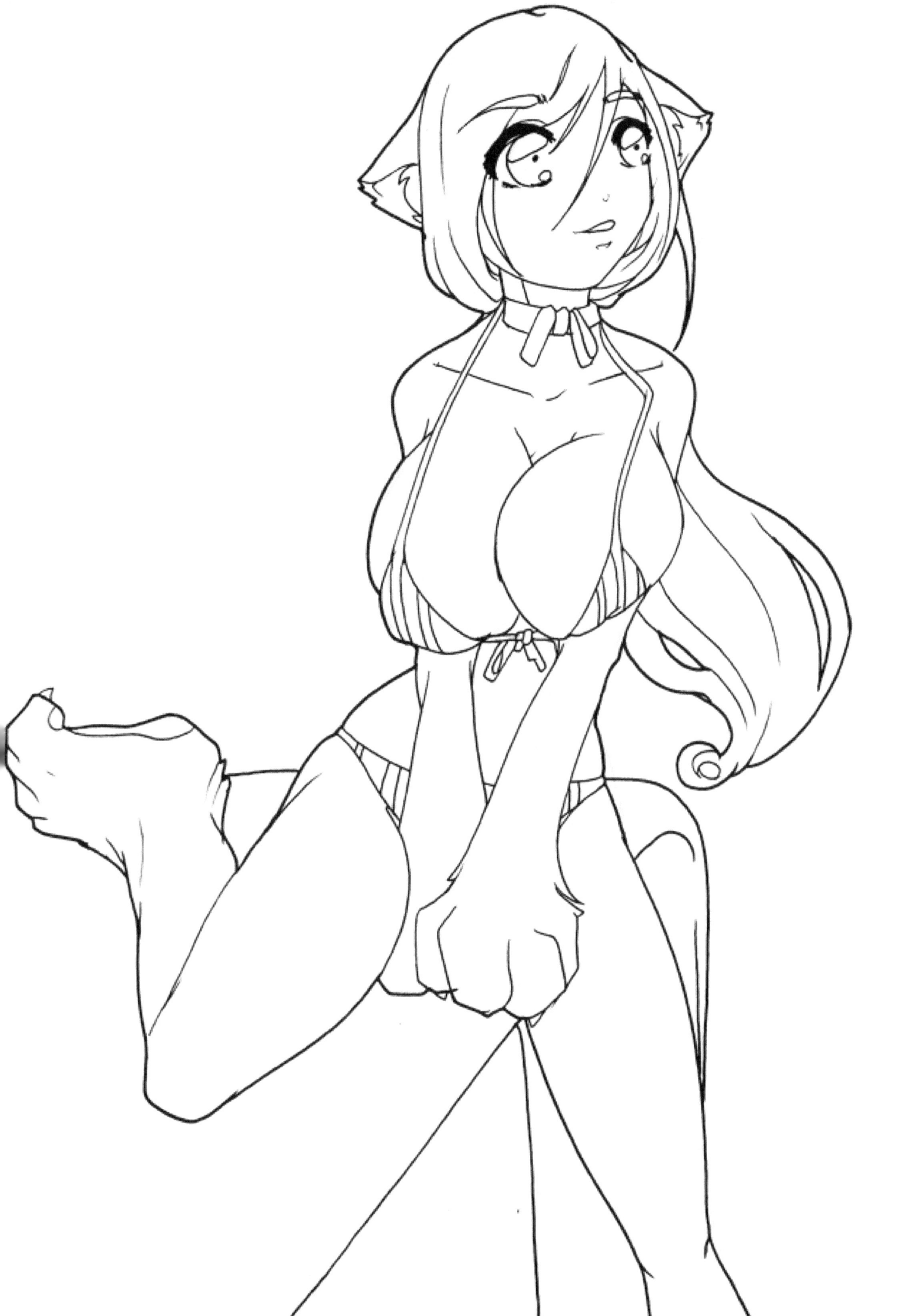

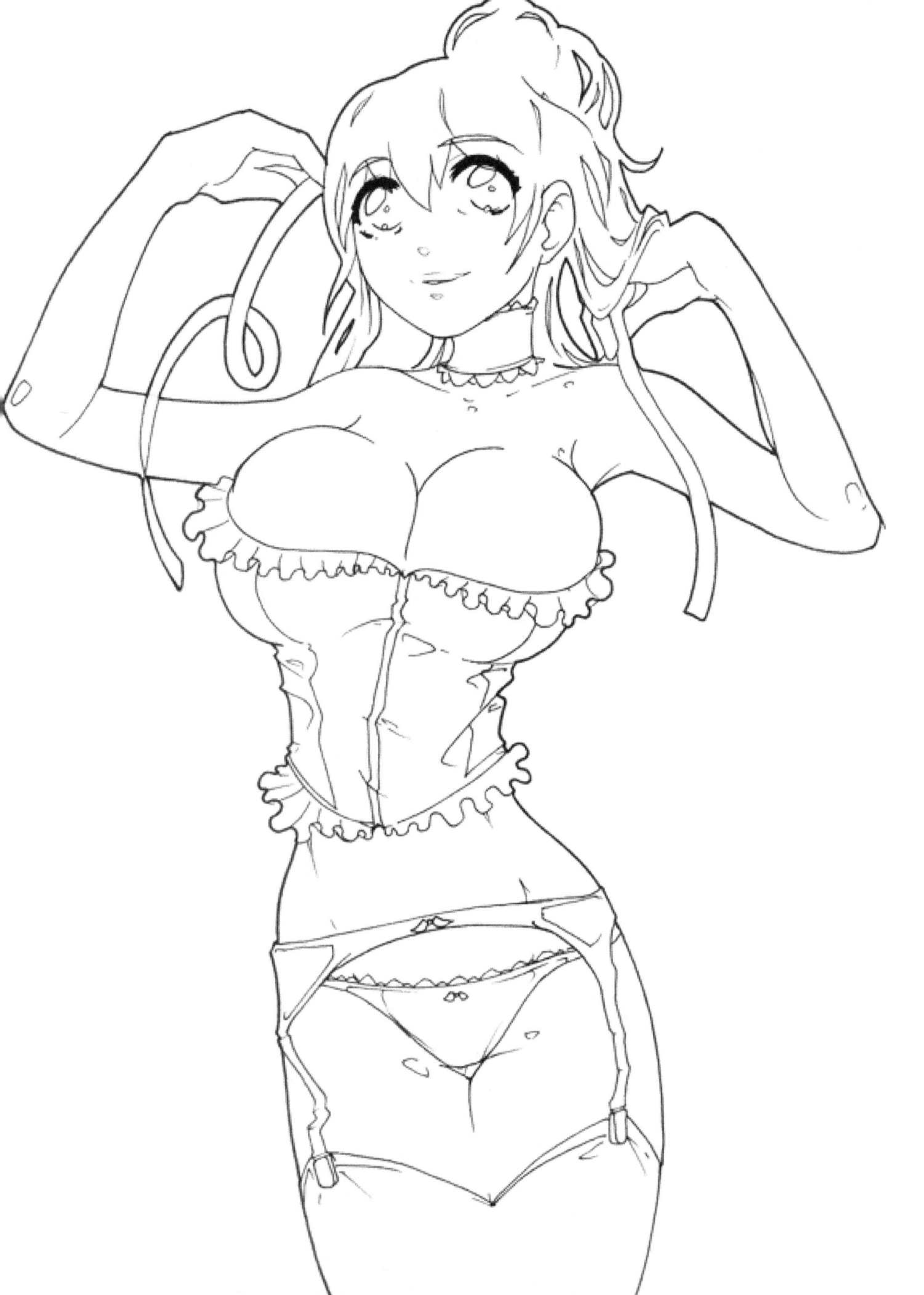

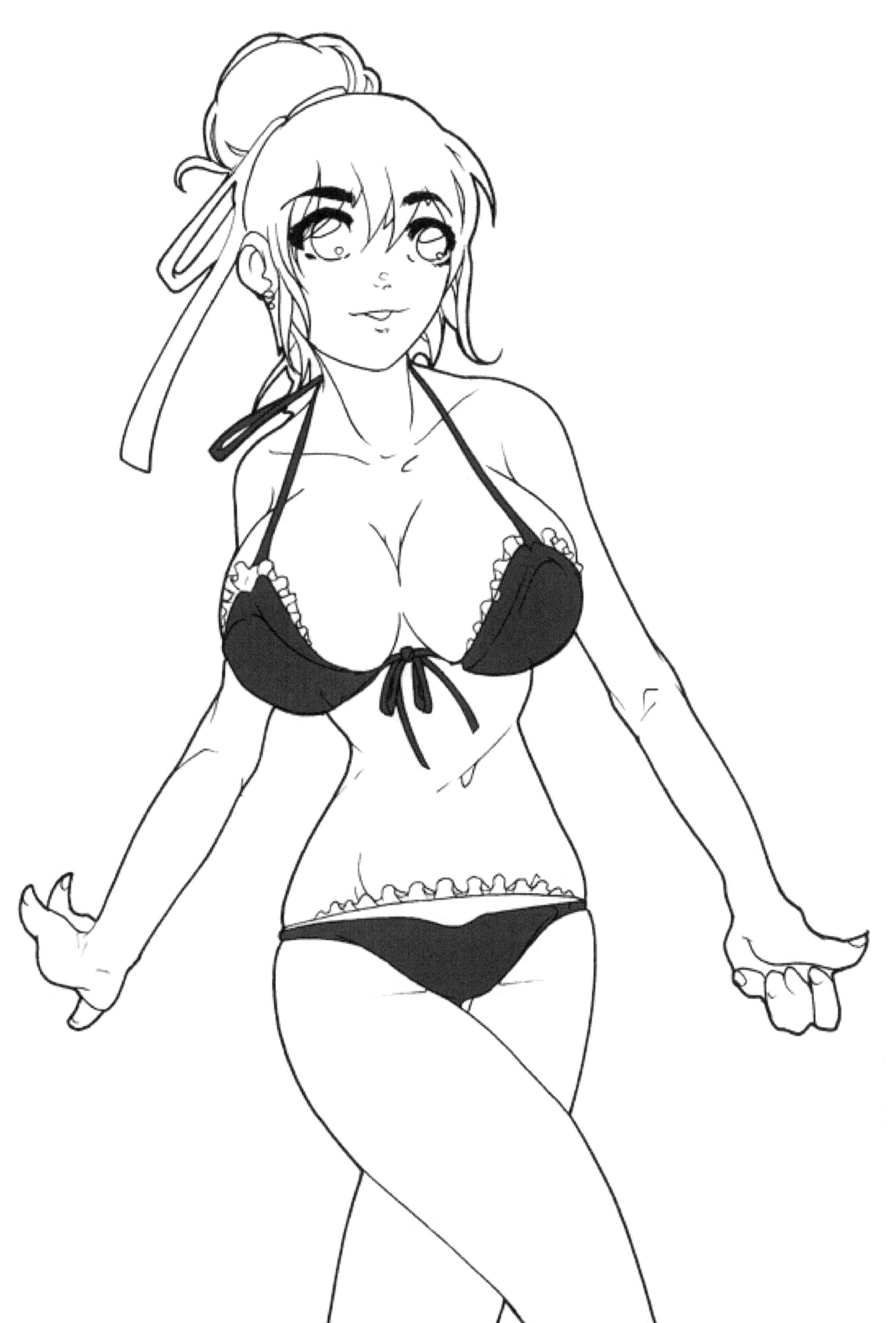

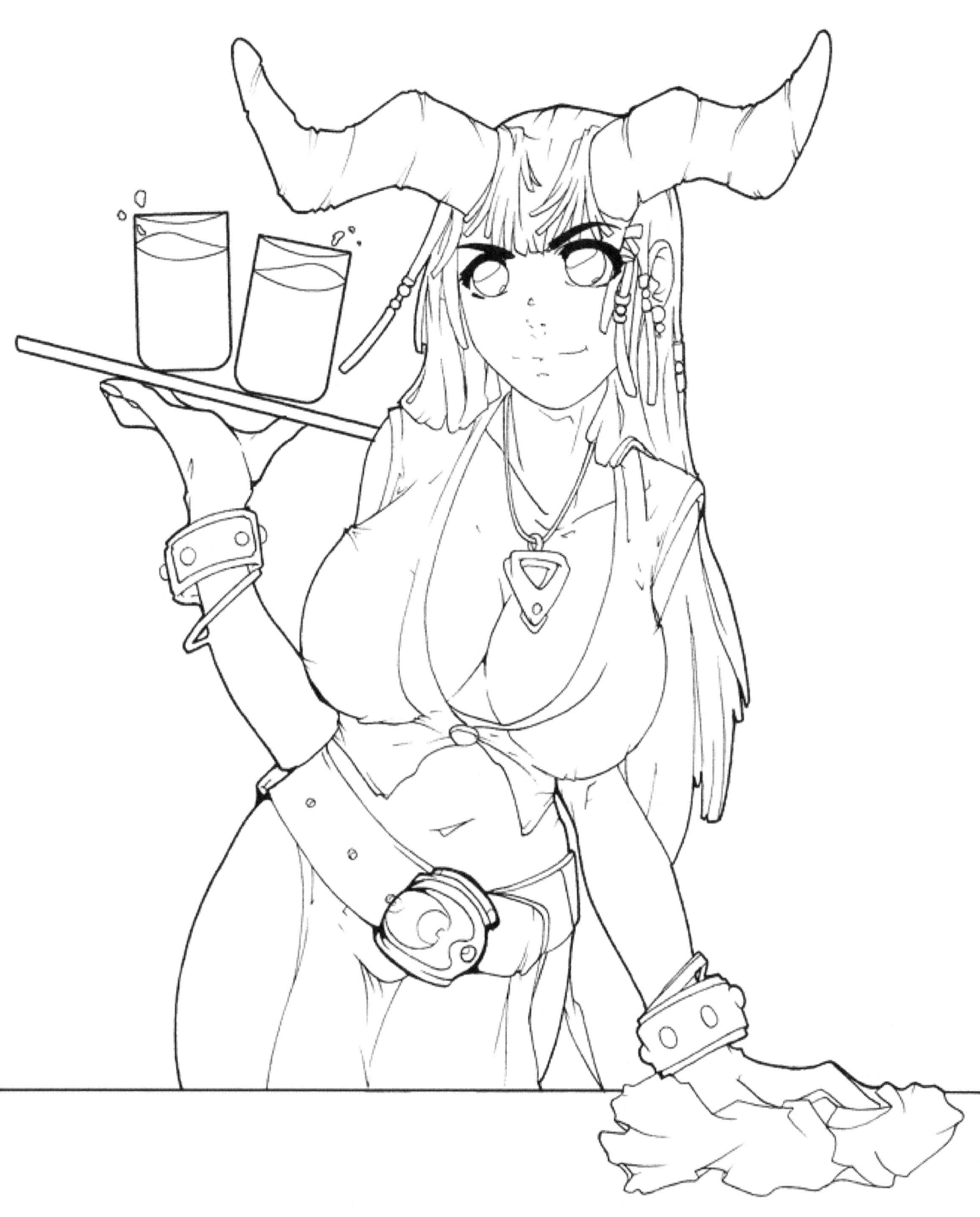

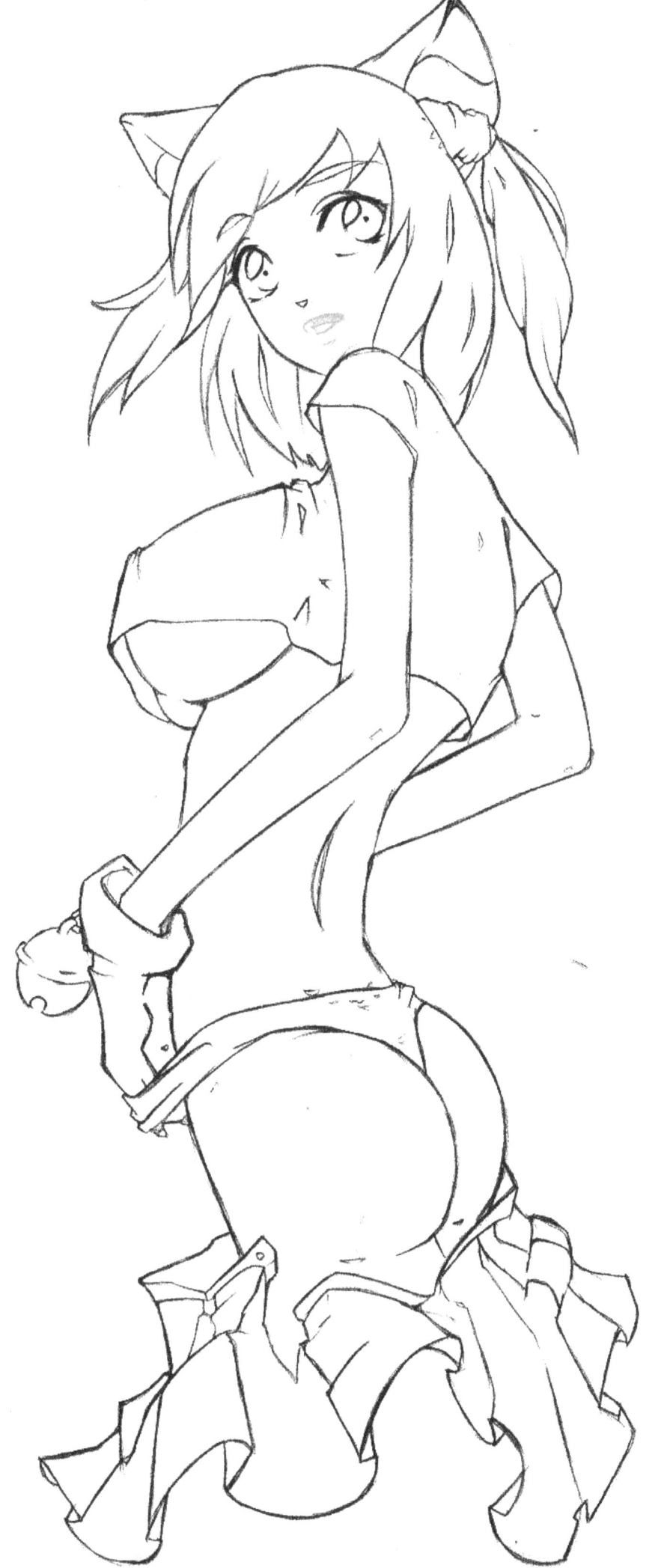

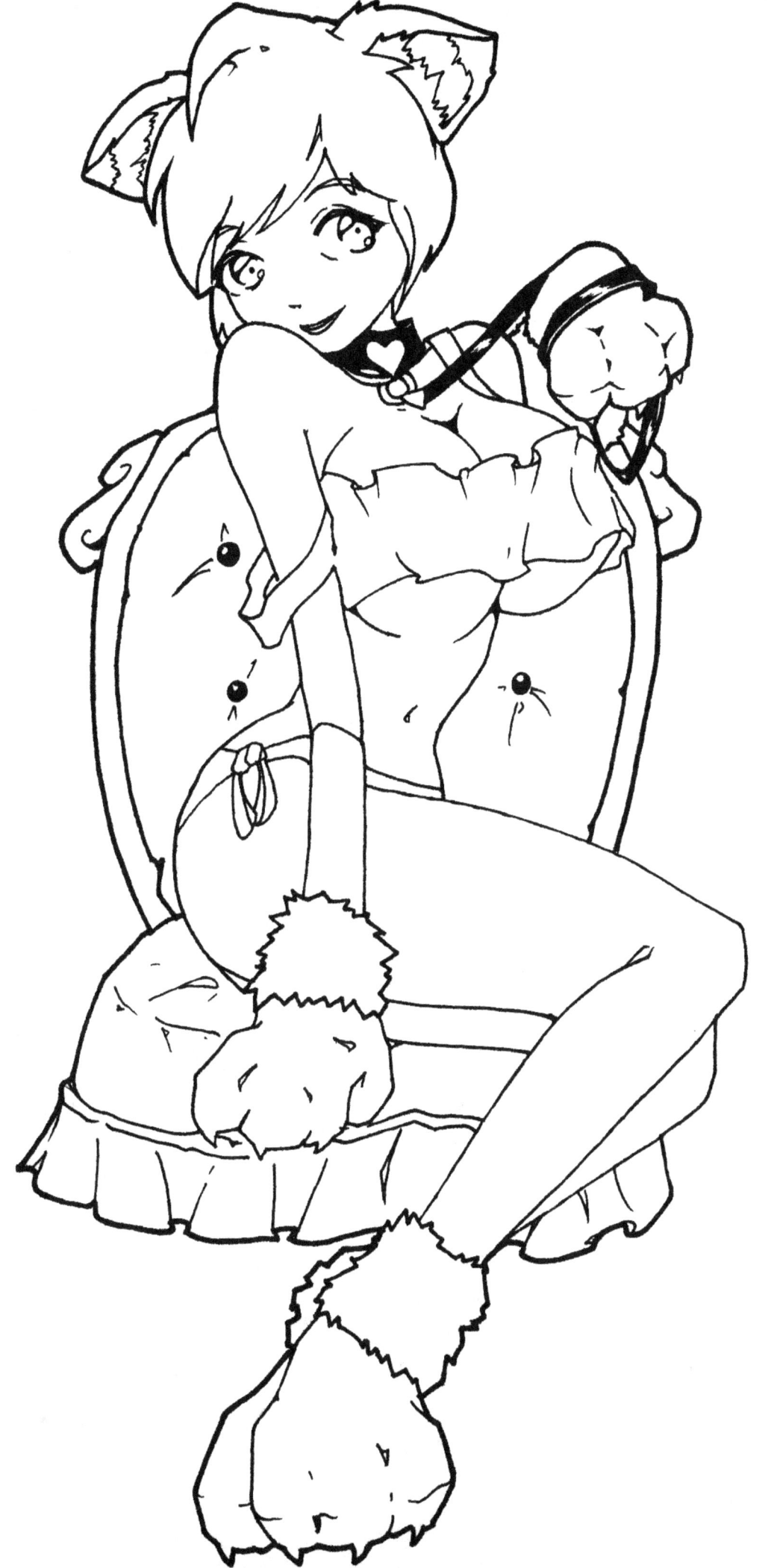

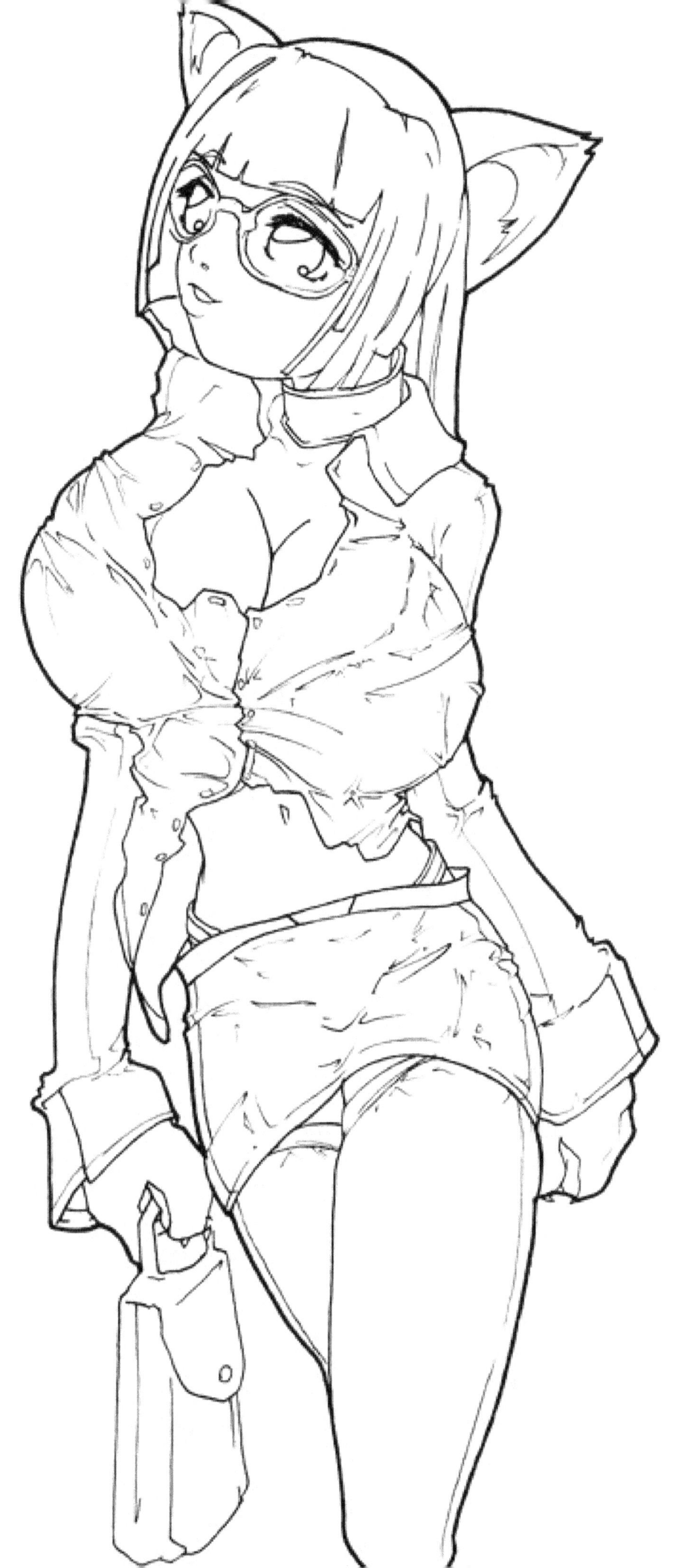

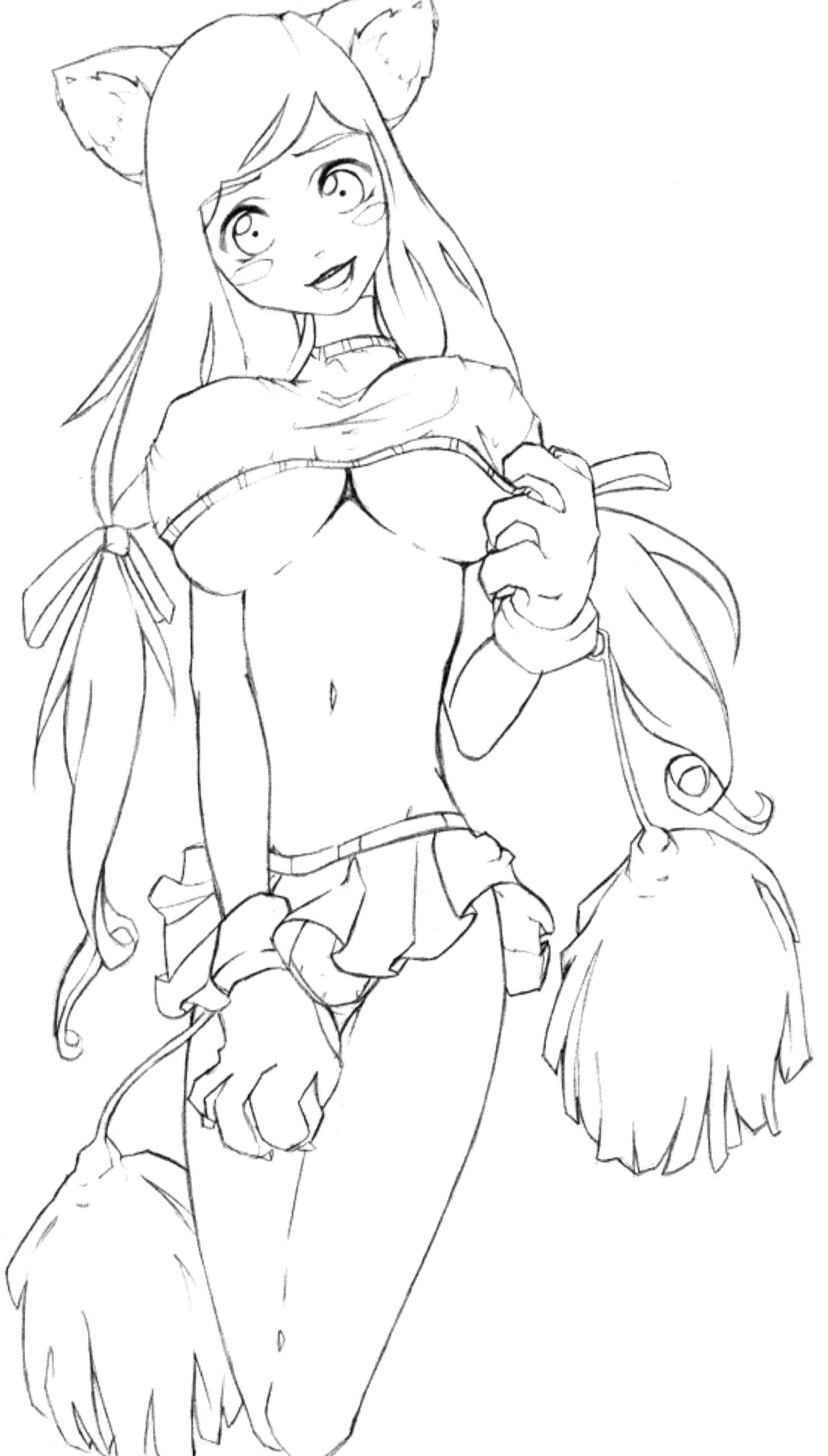

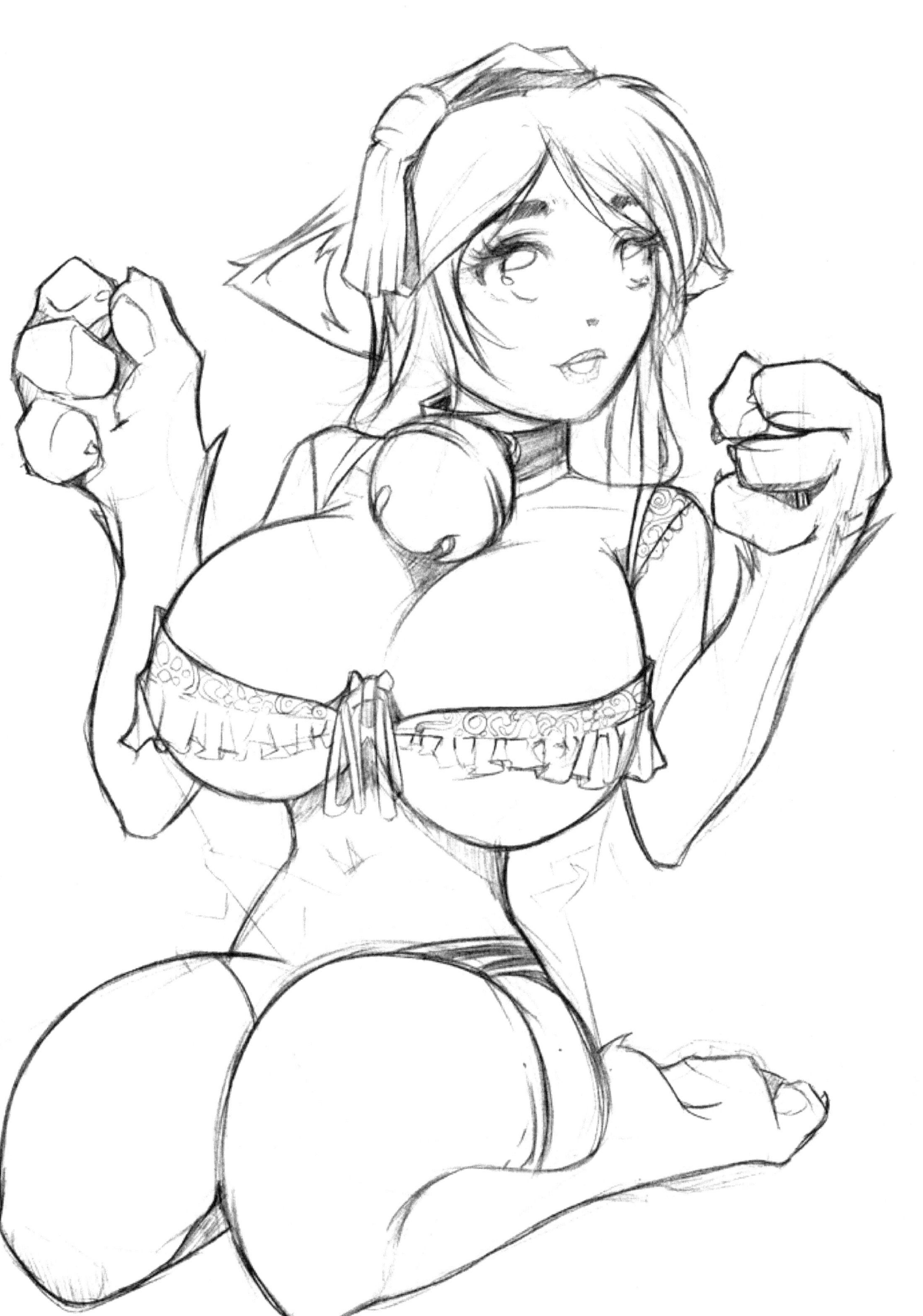

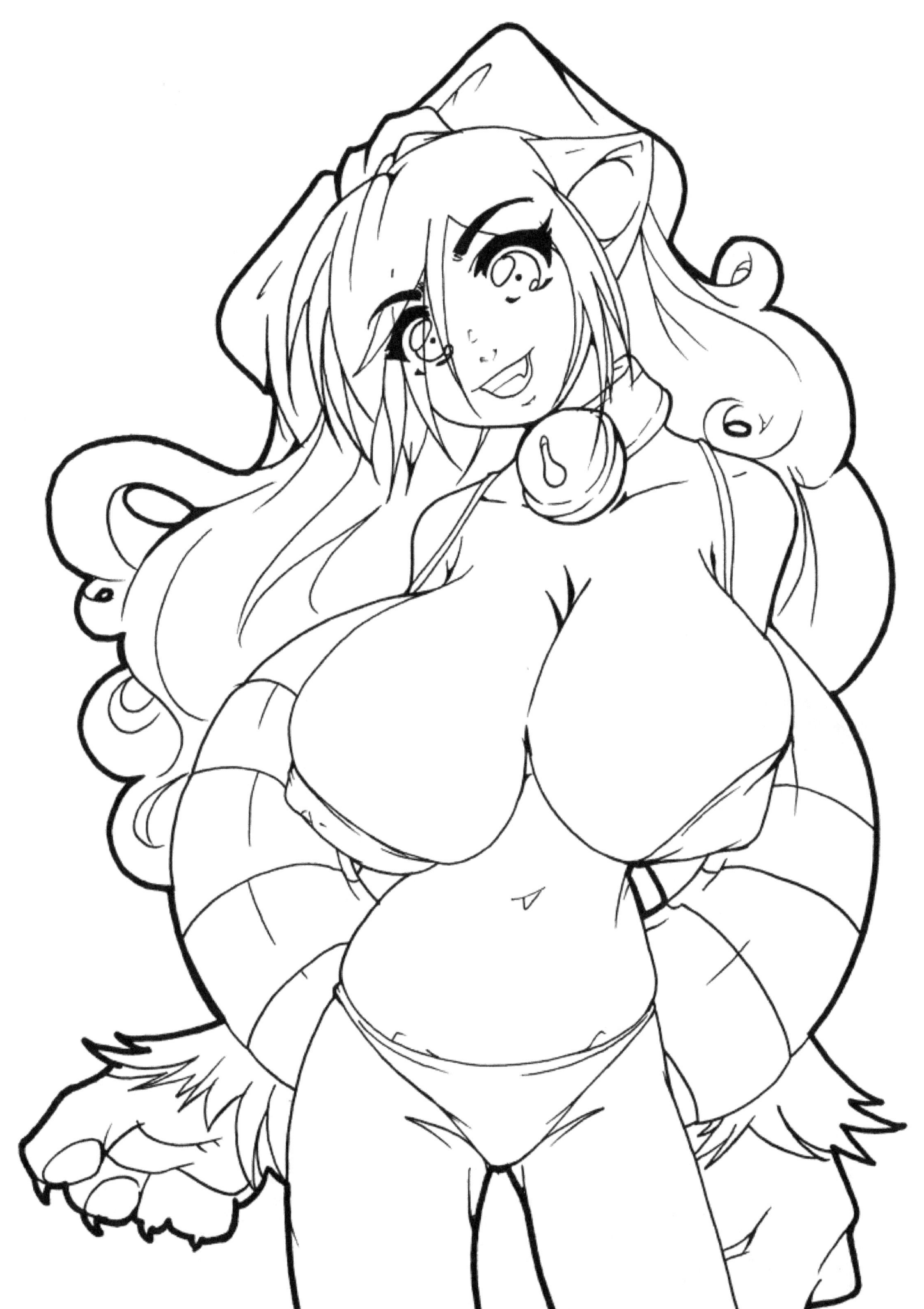

www.ingramcontent.com/pod-product-compliance
Lightning Source LLC
Chambersburg PA
CBHW060430220526
45465CB00008B/3086